SCOTTISH CASTLES

SAMPSON LLOYD
CAMERON BROWN

SCOTTISH CASTLES

SAMPSON LLOYD
CAMERON BROWN

SCOTTISH CASTLES

SAMPSON LLOYD & CAMERON BROWN

Published by
AAPPL Artists' and Photographers' Press Ltd.
Church Farm House, Wisley, Surrey GU23 6QL, UK
info@aappl.com   www.aappl.com

Sales and Distribution
UK and Export: Turnaround Publisher Services Ltd.
orders@turnaround-uk.com
Australia & New Zealand: Peribo Pty Ltd.
michael.coffey@peribo.com.au
South Africa: Trinity Books
trinity@iafrica.com

A catalogue record for this book is available from the British Library.

Trade hardback Edition ISBN 9781904332794
Collector's Edition ISBN 9781904332848

Design (contents and cover): Stefan Nekuda
office@nekuda.at

Printed in Malaysia by: Imago Publishing
info@imago.co.uk

Half title page: Glencassley
Title page: Edinburgh

Contents

3000 BC
The Neolithic village of Skara Brae established in Orkney.

1000-600 BC
Late Bronze Age people arrive in northern Britain from the Continent.

appx. 700 BC – 100 AD the Iron Age: also referred to as Celtic period.

Celtic Knot.

Celtic Stone.

84
The Romans reach Inverness, the northerly limit of their conquest of Britain: beginning of the Roman period.

121
Construction begins of stone-built Hadrian's Wall as a defensive barrier across northern Britain. It is defended by forts placed at strategic intervals and stretches from the Tyne to the Solway, a distance of 72 miles (116 kilometres).

141
Stretching from the Clyde to the Forth, turf-built Antonine Wall separating Caledonia to the north from Britannia to the south, acts as the northernmost defensive line for the Roman armies, but it will soon be abandoned as impractical.

150
Ptolemy refers to a group of five islands lying between what are now Scotland and Ireland, featuring stone structures known as *brochs*, a fortified dwelling. The best-preserved example remains at Mousa, Shetland.

296
The word pict used for the first time in Roman literature.

360
The word Scots (Scotti) first used in Roman literature, to describe a warlike tribe in Ireland.

409
The Romans depart leaving Scotland to be split between the Irish (Gaelic) Scots on the west coast, the Angles in Northumbria (south-east), Picts in the north-east and Celtic Britons in Cumbria and Strathclyde. The northern tribes, only recently having been conquered by the Romans, had continued to live an Iron Age life-style. Beginning of the Anglo-Saxon period.

367
Marcellinus of Rome identifies the Scotti and Picti as members of a "Barbarian conspiracy" to attack the northern frontier of the Empire in Britain.

382
Roman commander Magnus Maximus defeats the Picts.

History of Scotland

Pictish Symbols.

The early kings were warrior chiefs of the various tribes occupying the area now known as Scotland. The first one considered to have been King of Scotland is Kenneth I who takes the throne in 843. The names of the early rulers are generally not recorded, with the exception of the Pictish kings: a list of their names was chronicled in the early 8th century, and added to since from other sources. The dates in brackets are the year of death or deposing of the king – not all are known.

Kings & Queens of Scotland

During the Bronze and Iron ages the key defensive structure was the hillfort, an enclosure or palisade of wooden stakes on a raised area of ground or a cliff-top.

Traprain Law, a Bronze Age hillfort.

Broch

200 - 1000
All the tribes – Britons, Angles, Picts and Scots – build fortresses using natural features of the landscape. Except in the case of the brochs these are usually wooden structures, some known as crannogs.

A reconstruction of the pilings for a crannog in a loch.

Artist's impression of a crannog on an island.

Development of Castles

appx. 500
Fergus Mor, a royal Irish chieftain, arrives in Argyll and begins to unite the Scotti and the Dal Riata tribes who had been drifting into the area from Ireland for approximately one hundred years. A kingdom is established here which is independent of Ireland and of the rest of Scotland. Irish Gaelic replaces Celtic as the common language of Dalriada (the area in the west, around Islay, Jura and Arran, Argyll and beyond present-day Oban). All subsequent kings of Scotland traditionally see themselves as descended from Fergus Mor.

Pictland
Dalriada

appx. 550 – 750
Territorial fighting between the Scots (Dalriada), Northumbrians and Picts in the east.

563
Christianity introduced by St. Columba arriving in Iona from Ireland.

664
At the Synod of Whitby, in northern England, the Celtic Church is forced to adopt the rule of St. Peter and the Church of Rome rather than that of St. Columba.

685
The Picts, sorely pressed by both Celt and Gael, manage to defeat a force of invading Saxons at Nectansmere, but the Picts soon disappear from history.

800 - 850
Norsemen invade and settle in the north and on the western coasts. Until the 15th century the Orkneys, Hebrides and Shetland are subject to the Norwegian crown, and much of Scotland's west coast is nominally Norwegian though in reality under the control of Celtic-Norse descendants of the original raiders, until absorbed into Scotland in 1266.

843
Kenneth McAlpin unites the Scots and the Picts, the first step towards a united Scotland, a process not finally achieved until Duncan's reign some two hundred years later. The Pictish culture is finally extinguished. From this time until the late 13th century Scotland is often referred to by the Gaelic name Alba. Donald II (889-900) was the first king described as ri Alban – King of Alba – rather than as a king of a particular tribe.

Kenneth I
(Cináed mac Ailpín)

g forces
sing from
in attack
barton Rock

Drest	Nechtan (621)	Bridei (706)	Caustantin (820)	
Talorch	Cinioch (631)	Nechtan (724)	Oengus (834)	
Nechtun	Gartnait	Alpin (728)	Drest (834)	
Galan	Bridei	Drest (729)	Eogan (839)	approx 843-860 Kenneth I
Gartnait	Talorc (653)	Nechtan (732)	Uurad	approx 860-863 Donald I
Cailtram	Talorgan (657)	Onuist (761)	Bridei	863-877 Constantine I
Talorc	Gartnait (663)	Bridei (763)	Ciniod	877-878 Aed
Galam (580)	Drest (672)	Ciniod (775)	Bridei	878-889 Giric
Bridei (584)	Bridei (693)	Alpin (780)	Drest (843)	
Gartnait (601)	Taran (696)	Talorgan (782)	Drest's successor	
		Drest (787)	was Cinaed mac Alpin	The House of Alpin (or MacAlpin)
		Conall (789)	(Kenneth I), 35th king	889-900 Donald II
			of Dalriada but first	
			King of Scotland.	

Dun Anlaimh Crannog built on an island in Loch Cinneachan reached by a 90-foot stone causeway.

From around 500 - 900AD Dunnad was the capital of Dalriada.

On Islay, Loch Allallaidh Crannog was built on an artificial island.

Malcolm I
(Máel Coluim mac Domnaill)

Malcolm II
(Máel Coluim mac Cináeda)

1005
Malcolm II kills Kenneth III and becomes king and continues the unification of Alba, Moray and Lothian.

1034
Duncan I (Donnchad) becomes the first king of a united Scotland.

1040
Macbeth kills Duncan and becomes king.

appx. 950 – 1000
The period from the accession of Malcolm I (943) to Malcolm II (1005) is marked by good relations with the Wessex rulers of England, and by internal dynastic disunity. Having invaded Cumbria in 945, King Edmund of England then gifts the province to Malcolm I on condition of a permanent alliance. Malcolm I takes control of the former Pictish / Viking kingdom of Moray.

Around 960
The Scots take Edinburgh and establish their first foothold in Lothian, then still part of the Saxon kingdom of Northumbria.

1080
Malcolm III reluctantly accepts the rule of the Normans and his son, David, given as a hostage after Malcolm's defeat by invading Normans, is brought up at the Norman court in London. After David's accession to the Scottish throne some estates in Scotland are granted to Norman families and to Gaelic lords prepared to offer support to the Anglo-Normans. The Norman system of feudal government is gradually introduced and tension grows between the native Scots and the ruling classes, seen as puppets of the Normans and out of touch with their own people. Violent rebellion continues until well into the 13th century, particularly in outlying regions.

Panel one of the Bayeux Tapestry showing the English setting out to defend the realm against the Norman invaders.

Constantine II

The House of Alpin (continued)
900-943 Constantine II

The House of Dunkeld
943-954 Malcolm I
954-962 Indulf
962-967 Dubh
967-971 Cuilean
971-995 Kenneth II
995-997 Constantine III
997-1005 Kenneth III
1005-1034 Malcolm II
1034-1040 Duncan I
1040-1057 Macbeth
1057-1058 Lulach (The Fool)

The House of Canmore
1058-1093 Malcolm III (Canmore)
1093-1094 Donald Ban
May-Nov. 1094 Duncan II
1094-1097 Donald Ban and Edmund
1097-1107 Edgar (The Peaceable)

This section of the Bayeux Tapestry shows an attack on Dinan in Northern France. The fort, surrounded by a wooden palisade and set on a hill is a model for the motte & bailey structures which the Normans soon introduce to Scotland.

1107
Break-up of united Scotland with Alexander I as king of the Scots and David I king of Lothian and Strathclyde.

1124
Unity restored on Alexander's death with David I becoming sole King of Scots. His reign is one of the most important in Scotland's history, extending Scottish borders to the River Tees, including all of Northumberland and introducing Norman political structures.

A carving of a galley of the type which Somerled would have used.

1164
Somerled, King of the Isles, a nobleman of Norse and Celtic descent, and founder of the dynasty of Lords of the Isles, is killed by the Stewarts at a battle in Renfrewshire. His three sons divide the kingdom between them but it officially becomes part of Scotland in 1266. Somerled's three sons are the founders of the clans MacDougall, MacDonald and McRory and their descendants remain powerful chieftain-barons, particularly during Scotland's crisis years following the death of Alexander III in 1286 without an accepted successor, and in the Wars of Independence.

1165-74
William the Lion makes an alliance between Scotland and France but is ultimately obliged to break that treaty and subject Scotland to English rule, a treaty revoked 15 years later by Richard the Lionheart.

1286
On his death Alexander III is succeeded by his daughter, The Maid of Norway. She is betrothed to Edward I's son but dies on the journey from Norway, leaving Edward I to adjudicate between the various claimants to the Scottish crown.

John de Balliol and his wife.

1296-1358
The Wars of Independence. Edward I chooses John de Balliol as King of Scotland but he is rejected by William Wallace and then Robert the Bruce, who defeats the English under Edward II at Bannockburn in 1314.

Scottish kings from ancient times were crowned on the Stone of Destiny. In 1296 Edward I had Balliol crowned on the stone, then removed it to England. It is seen here beneath the Coronation Throne in Westminster Abbey. It was returned to Scotland in 1996.

The House of Canmore (continued)
1107-1124 Alexander I (The Fierce)
1124-1153 David I
1153-1165 Malcolm IV (The Maiden)
1165-1214 William (The Lion)
1214-1249 Alexander II
1249-1286 Alexander III

The House of Balliol
1292-1296 John de Balliol

1296-1306 The Second Interregnum

1286-1290 Margaret (Maid of Norway)

(1290-1292) The First Interregnum

The great seal of Alexader II

1100 - 1200
Construction of Norman–influenced motte & bailey castles.

Artist's impression of a motte.

1200
Stone structures begin to replace earlier wooden ones and the first use of curtain walls seen in the west of Scotland.

Castle Sween

1250 - 1300
Development of castle complexes, with tower, keep and gatehouse.

1260
End of the Norse influence in the west.

1295/6
The start of the Wars of Scottish Independence with many major castles seized by the forces of Edward I of England or those Scottish nobles who sided with him.

1297/8 Many of the same castles liberated by William Wallace

1320
The Pope accepts The Declaration of Arbroath, confirming Scotland's independence from England.

1326
Robert the Bruce convenes what might be described as Scotland's first parliament.

1332 - 38
Edward III invades Scotland to support Balliol's son's claim to the crown and is backed by the Lord of the Isles, and his Clan Donald.

Robert the Bruce.   David II with Edward III.

1396
In this year, in Perth, before the king and his court, Europe's last trial by combat takes place, between feuding clans unable to settle their differences. In the words of Walter Scott in *The Fair Maid of Perth:*
The trumpets of the King sounded a charge, the bagpipes blew up their screaming and maddening notes, and the combatants, starting forward in regular order, and increasing their pace, till they came to a smart run, met together in the centre of the ground, as a furious land torrent encounters an advancing tide. Blood flowed fast, and the groans of those who fell began to mingle with the cries of those who fought. The wild notes of the pipes were still heard above the tumult and stimulated to further exertion the fury of the combatants. At once, however, as if by mutual agreement, the instruments sounded a retreat. The two parties disengaged themselves from each other to take breath for a few minutes. About twenty of both sides lay on the field, dead or dying; arms and legs lopped off, heads cleft to the chin, slashes deep through the shoulder to the breast, showed at once the fury of the combat, the ghastly character of the weapons used, and the fatal strength of the arms which wielded them.
Of the sixty combatants only 12 survived.

1371
Robert II, grandson of Robert the Bruce, is crowned as the first Stewart king of Scotland. (NB. Stewart is the original Scottish spelling of the name. Mary Queen of Scots and her descendants adopted the French form Stuart.) Margaret, daughter of Robert the Bruce, was married to Walter Stewart, High Steward of Scotland. The family name derived from the title, first granted to the family by Davd I, some 200 years previously. Margaret died giving birth to Robert II, who becomes king 54 years after her death. He has two wives, several mistresses and sires 21 children.
During his reign, and that of his son Robert III, the troubles with England continue, with Henry IV invading Scotland in 1400. At one stage Robert's son, the future James I, is captured by pirates whilst on a journey to France, is handed to the English and remains 18 years a prisoner. On his father's death he is ransomed and assumes the throne at age 21. He is ultimately murdered by a group of his own, disaffected barons.

The House of Bruce
1306-1329 Robert I (The Bruce)
1329-1371 David II

The House of Stewart / Stuart
1371-1390 Robert II

1390-1406 Robert III
Robert changes his name from John upon his accession to the throne, believing his own name would remind people of the puppet king, John Balliol, and be a source of bad luck. There is a question mark over the legitimacy of his birth and his brother, christened Robert, wields significant influence over the king. Robert III suggests that he be buried in a dungheap and that his own epitaph should be: *Here lies the worst of kings and the most wretched of men in the whole kingdom.*

The coat of arms of the House of Stewart.

Robert III was buried at Paisley Abbey, feeling he did not deserve the honour of interment at Scone.

1300/05
Edward I re-takes key Scottish strongholds.

1350 – 1400
First fortified tower houses built.

1308 - 1329
Robert the Bruce systematically damages castles throughout the land to prevent their use by the English. During this period castles are again re-taken by the Scots with Stirling liberated after the Battle of Bannockburn in 1314.

1332 - 1338
Edward III's invasion results in major damage to many castles.

Hermitage   Caerlaverock   Stirling

1460
James II is killed at siege of Roxburgh by an exploding cannon. This is the first time that cannon are used in Britain. Roxburgh was a former Scottish royal castle now occupied by the English. The castle is destroyed at the siege.

James III

James IV was 15 years old when he fought against his father at the Battle of Sauchieburn in 1488.

1460-88
James III promotes alliance with England, which makes him unpopular at home and is, in any case, unsuccessful, as Edward IV invades (unsuccessfully) in 1482. James is eventually killed in battle against an army of disaffected nobles, including his own son, the future James IV.

1502
James IV marries a daughter of Henry VII of England and signs the treaty of perpetual peace with England.

1505
Construction of Scotland's first printing press.

1513
Henry VIII declares war on France, and Scotland sides with France and invades England. James IV is killed at Flodden Field and succeeded by his one-year-old son James V. For the next 30 years the Borders become the scene of constant harassment by the English and the local barons are encouraged to strengthen existing castles or build new ones.

1542
Mary Queen of Scots assumes the throne at the death of James V: she is one week old.

1544 - 45
Henry VIII tries to force a marriage between his son and the infant Mary, and makes damaging incursions into the Border country. This has become known as "the rough wooing".

1544 - 1603
This period is is one of the great moments in Scots' history. In 1548 Mary is sent to France for safekeeping and eventually marries the Dauphin, who becomes king of France in 1559. In 1560 the Reformation is proclaimed and a year later Mary returns, following the death of her husband. She marries Darnley, great-grandson of Henry VII. He is murdered and two years later she marries Bothwell, but is soon imprisoned in Leven Castle and forced to abdicate in favour of her son James (aged one year). In 1587, after 18 years of imprisonment by Elizabeth I of England, Mary is executed at Fotheringay.

Mary Queen of Scots.

The House of Stewart / Stuart (continued)
1406-1437 James I
　　　　1437-1460 James II
　　　　　　1460-1488 James III
　　　　　　　　1488-1513 James IV
　　　　　　　　　　1513-1542 James V
　　　　　　　　　　　　1542-1567 Mary Queen of Scots
　　　　　　　　　　　　1567-1625 James VI

1400 - 1450
Rise of powerful nobles and associated development of baronial strongholds. Central towers added to curtain wall castles in the west.

1450 - 1550
Royal castles built or strengthened to withstand artillery fire, first used at the siege of Roxburgh castle in 1460. Older castles such as Dunbar and Urquhart modernized.

Urquhart Castle

1550 - 1600
Further evolution of the tower house style.

Crathes

Cawdor

Craigston

1603
Elizabeth I dies and James VI of Scotland is crowned James I of England – the Union of the Crowns.

1625
Charles I becomes king.

1638
The signing of the National Covenant is designed as a protest against the English crown and church hierarchy who have been trying for years to unify the prayer-books of the English and Scottish churches. In 1642 the English civil war begins and the Covenantors raise forces to help the Parliamentarians. In Scotland the Earl of Montrose sides with Charles I so the civil war spreads to Scotland.

1649
The execution of Charles I.

1650
Charles II is crowned in Scotland but flees the Cromwellian army and returns to England at the Restoration in 1660. Montrose is executed by the Marquess of Argyll.

1679
Defeat of the Covenantors by the Duke of Monmouth's forces at the Battle of Bothwell Brig.

1685
On the death of Charles II, James II and VII becomes the last Catholic king.

1688
The Glorious Revolution. Mainly because of his Catholicism James is rejected by political leaders of the day and William of Orange is invited from Holland to depose him. He accepts and takes the throne with James II's daughter Mary. In 1689 they pass the Bill of Rights, the first step in limiting the absolute powers of the monarchy.

1692
Glencoe Massacre. The MacDonalds, having refused allegiance to King William, are slaughtered by the Campbells.

The execution of Charles I in Whitehall, London, in 1649.

Glencoe, where the infamous massacre of 1692 took place.

1603
James became James VI of Scotland and I of England, uniting the crowns of both countries. Thereafter, all monarchs reign jointly over Scotland and England.

1625-1649 Charles I

1606
The Scottish saltire is incorporated into the first Union Flag.

1651-1659 The Commonwealth & Protectorate

1660 The House of Stewart / Stuart (restored)
1660-1685 Charles II (crowned at Scone 1650, exiled and restored 1660)
1685-1688 James VII
1689-1702 William III & Mary II. Mary Stuart dies 1694.
William also known as William II of Scotland and as William of Orange.

William III

1600 – 1660
Building of grand castles for government officers and end of the era of tower house building.

Craigievar

1650 – 1700
Many castles are destroyed or damaged in the fighting between Covenantors, Parliamentarians and the Royalists.

1660 - 1715
First classical mansions built – Thirlestane, Floors, Drumlanrig.

Brodie Castle, partly destroyed in 1645.

Thirlestane

Drumlanrig

1707
Great Britain comes into being on the dissolution of the two separate Scottish and English parliaments and the creation of a combined government at Whitehall.

1714
Death of the last Stuart monarch, Queen Anne, succeeded by the first of the Hanoverians, George I.

1715 – 1746
A series of Jacobite (supporters of King James and the Stuarts) uprisings against the Hanoverian rule, culminating in defeat at the battle of Culloden, and the escape of Bonnie Prince Charlie (Charles Edward Stuart) to France.

Bonnie Prince Charlie

appx. 1760 – 1845
The Highland Clearances. Tens of thousands of men, women and children evicted, often violently, from their homes to make way for large scale sheep farming and driven to a harsh subsistence existence on the coasts or emigration, generally to England or to the colonies.

1822
George IV becomes the first monarch since Charles II to make an official visit to Scotland.

1852
Queen Victoria purchases Balmoral.

Balmoral

1996
The Stone of Destiny returns to Scotland to be kept in Edinburgh Castle.

1885
The post of Secretary (later – Secretary of State) for Scotland is created in Parliament.

1918
Votes for women (aged 30 or more) introduced.

1934
Formation of the Scottish National Party (SNP): the first SNP member of parliament is elected in 1945.

1947
The first Edinburgh Festival is held.

1999
The devolved Scottish parliament sits for the first time.

1702-1714 Anne
The accession of the House of Hanover in 1714 ends the line of Scottish monarchs that stretched back almost 900 years and introduces the German line whose descendants still rule today.

Kings and Queens of the United Kingdom
The House of Hanover
1714-1727 George I
1727-1760 George II
1760-1820 George III

1820-1830 George IV
1830-1837 William IV
1837-1901 Victoria

The House of Saxe-Coburg
1901-1910 Edward VII
1910-1936 George V

The House of Windsor (from 1917)
1910-1936 George V
1936 Edward VIII
1936-1952 George VI
1952- Elizabeth II

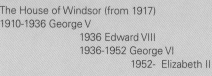

The coat of arms of the House of Hanover.

The coat of arms of Saxe-Coburg-Gotha.

The coat of arms of the House of Windsor.

1719
Eilean Donan destroyed by Spanish invaders

1746 - Last siege of a castle in Britain, at Blair Castle.

1750 - 1850
Evolution of the Scottish Baronial and Gothic styles, at Blair, Balmoral (rebuilt by Victoria and Albert), Dunvegan, Inverary and others.

Eilean Donan

Blair Castle

Glamis

Dunvegan

Perhaps the grandest of Scotland's castles, Stirling was the favourite residence of many of the Stuart monarchs.
There has been a castle on this site for almost 1,000 years.

Introduction

What do we mean by a "castle"? Most of us, asked to picture a Scottish castle, would probably think of Edinburgh or Stirling or a tall, rectangular stone house, perhaps whitewashed, with projecting round towers with conical slate roofs at the corners. Yet there is no one style which accurately represents each era or region and much of what we see today as typically historic Scottish is actually an invention of the 19th century, when Queen Victoria's love affair with Balmoral turned the Highlands into a very fashionable part of the country.

There have been fortified buildings in Scotland for thousands of years but by the time of William the Conqueror's invasion of Scotland in 1072 there was still no tradition of castle-building in its "modern" form, which is a Norman introduction. The older examples of castles which we can still see are largely the result of the constant skirmishing and fighting between clans, with invaders from Scandinavia and with English armies and brigands over the centuries following a relatively peaceful period of co-existence with the first of the Norman aristocrats. The more recent ones are simply evidence of the Scots' ongoing fascination for this type of building. King David I of Scotland (ruled 1124 – 1153) is credited as the first builder of castles in the region – *He it is that has decked thee [Scotland] with castles and towns, and with lofty towers.* (John of Fordun, C14th Scots chronicler.) David's sister Matilda was the wife of Henry I and he himself spent ten years living in England and soaking up Norman influences before returning with a Norman wife and retinue to take up the throne of Scotland and begin the process of change in his kingdom.

Over the course of the 11th and 12th centuries two distinct categories of castle were built, the royal castles, and those owned by feudal barons and knights, who received land from the crown in exchange for their military support. Royal castles, including Edinburgh, Stirling, Jedburgh, Roxburgh and Peebles, were where the royal family resided and ruled as they travelled around the land. They lived from the proceeds of rents paid locally – often in kind – and the seat of government at any one time was the place where the king was currently staying. Eventually they became permanent outposts of local government, each the headquarters of an administrative region – a *shire* or *sherrifdom* – the home of the sherrif, local law-court and prison. There was a stone-built castle in Edinburgh as early as Malcolm II's time (1058-1093), and Alexander I died in Stirling Castle in 1124, but there is no record of what these buildings looked like. We can presume that the Scottish kings of the day will have had some knowledge of the castle-building going on south of the border and even in other parts of Europe, but no records remain of these early castles and it seems clear that the main catalyst for castle-building was the arrival of the Normans.

The incoming Norman aristocracy and those local nobles who accepted the new order of things began to build castles or fortified houses in order to provide

This *broch* is less than one mile from Dunrobin castle in Sutherland.

the defensive garrisons which were the price they paid for their grant of land from the king. The most prominent of the new aristocracy themselves made grants of smaller parcels of their estates to others in return for their military support at a local level: these grantees were called *knights* and they were also expected to build castles. Robert the Bruce's ancestor Robert de Brus was a senior member of the Norman aristocracy and in 1124 was given the lordship of Annandale in the Borders, in exchange for the services of ten knights and their armies.

The most basic form of Norman castle was the *motte and bailey* structure, the *motte* being a natural or man-made mound and the *bailey* the enclosed courtyard below. This structure can be seen in the Bayeux Tapestry and there is evidence of over 300 of them in Scotland, despite the fact that they were generally built of wood. Their simplicity was of course advantageous as all the builders required was fit labour, timber and basic carpentry skills and the whole thing could be finished and inhabited in a matter of weeks. They seem to have been used predominantly in areas of political unrest, where defence was paramount and a building could be put up very quickly. A good example which can still be seen today is the Bass of Inverurie, in Aberdeenshire, built in the late 1100s. Much of Scotland was peaceful during the immediate aftermath of the Norman conquest and another form of castle, the *ringwork*, offering fewer defensive characteristics was also popular in this part of Britain. This consisted of robust free-standing houses of timber or stone, built perhaps on a small elevation but often on the same level as the surrounding land, and encircled by a defensive ditch or earthwork. A large example

Castle Sween is one of the earliest of the surviving stone castles and can be dated to the late 1100s.

of a ringwork, with a 90-foot (27-metre) diameter and surrounded by a ditch, has been excavated in Glasgow near to the cathedral.

At the same time as the Norman influence was pervading the borders and central regions the Norse culture remained firmly entrenched on the west coast and in the Northern Isles, still under Norwegian rule. Norse sagas of the 12th and 13th centuries tell of castles and *borgs* and at least some of these are clearly contemporary stone structures. As kings of Norway went on pilgrimages to Jerusalem as early as 1107 it is not surprising that they should have picked up architectural influences quite different from their own tradition of fortified wooden halls. On the other hand, there was plenty of stone and not many trees in the Orkneys and Caithness so the change was perhaps inevitable. Certainly there seems at this early stage to have been more building in stone in the far north and west than there was in the rest of Scotland.

Castle Sween is one of the earliest of the surviving stone castles and can be dated to the late 1100s. It was built by Sven (in Gaelic *Suibhne* – pronounced Sween) the Red on a rocky ridge beside Loch Sween by Jura Sound on the west coast. Sven was a warlord with a mix of Celtic, Norse and Gaelic blood in his veins but his castle shows clear Norman influence in its use of buttresses and its style of doorway. Another fine and, perhaps more typical example of the period, is Tioram in Loch Moidart, standing on a rocky promontory which is covered at high tide. The curtain wall on the seaward side rises to over 60 feet (18 metres) and is over 6 feet (2 metres) thick, and is not buttressed. This was the stronghold of

Ardvreck was built in 1490 by the MacLeods of Assynt and the ruins stand at the east end of Loch Assynt, in the Highlands.

Dun Dornaigil is a ruined *broch* in Sutherland. It has an intramural staircase within its 4.5 metre thick walls, and would have been some 7 metres high.

clan MacRuari, also of Norse ancestry. Duart on Mull and Dunvegan on Skye are two further examples of this castle style. Interestingly none of these early castles has arrow-slits or other openings in the defensive outer walls: their sole means of protection was inaccessibility, height and the thickness of the walls themselves.

Scottish fortified building dates back at least to the Iron Age and the prefix Dun-, attached to many of the medieval castles (Dunvegan, Dun Ringill etc), refers back to an earlier *dun* (fortified hill). It is quite possible that a *broch* may once have stood on the same site. Brochs are something of a mystery. The term is used to describe stone buildings, generally circular, of very basic construction. So few survive with much of the structure intact that archeologists and historians struggle to agree what their function really was. Were they defensive forts, homes for successful farmers, or simply strong stone houses built to a common pattern? They were certainly very evident in the far north but are also found down in the Borders. Some were not far removed from simple huts while others boasted double walls, with stairways between. There is every indication that this kind of building was used for many centuries in Scotland, but nowhere else in Europe, from at least 100 BC, and probably much earlier, with the last examples dating to around 300 AD. Brochs which can be visited today include Mousa Broch (the walls here are well preserved, standing some 40 feet (13 metres) high), Clickimin, Levenwick and Culswick in Shetland; Dun Carloway on Lewis; Gurness and Midhowe in Orkney; and on the mainland, Dun Trodden and Dun Telve (both in Glenelg) and Dun Dornaigil in Sutherland.

Whatever the brochs' past function it is certain that some of the later castles were built on the sites of these earlier structures, and that at least some of the brochs will, through their location, have had strategic defensive importance. Dunnad is on a site dating from the Iron Age period, but is most famous as being the stronghold of the Scotti tribe and centre of the Kingdom of Dalriada (*Dal Riata*). The Scotti tribe were invaders from Ireland in the 5th and 6th centuries AD and their name is the origin of the name *Scotland*.

In the era preceding the construction of the brochs we have hill-forts, such as Traprain Law in East Lothian, dating back as far as the Iron Age. These are fortresses protected by earthen ditches with stone walls or wooden palisades or stockades, and built on hill tops or on coastal promontories. Hill-forts were designed to defend against raiding parties with weapons of bronze and, later, iron and the availability of horses, but they also served as status symbols for the local chieftain. From their hill-forts these warrior lords could control the surrounding areas and offer safety to the people who farmed the land and who looked to their chieftain for protection. Scotland was not an organized or unified country at this time in history but the appearance of these settlements on the landscape indicates the development of a relatively structured and hierarchical society, where the power of chieftains was increasing along with the need of their people for protection.

There were two main reasons for the spate of castle-building following the calm years after the Norman invasion: continuing fighting with the Norsemen in the west and the northern isles and the Wars of Independence against the English.

In the 13th century the Norwegians finally lost control of the western coast but not before a series of raids and battles had become the catalyst for a surge of castle-building by the Scots. The great local warrior clans - the MacDougalls, MacDonalds, MacLachlans, MacSweens and Lamonts - all proud and independent, all built at this time, and many of their and their neighbours' structures survive to this day.

In the first millennium Scotland was affected more by internal strife than by conflict with its neighbours to the south. The arrival of the Normans introduced a period of relative peace to the Borders and central regions, but the period of strong Scottish monarchy ended with the death in 1286 of the Maid of Norway, the heir to Alexander III. Rival claimants to the throne appeared but Edward I of England installed his puppet king, Balliol, and the Wars of Independence under Wallace (Braveheart) and Robert the Bruce began.

Wooden houses, sufficient for times of comparative peace, had to be replaced by more substantial defensive structures. Whilst the Normans were building motte and bailey forts the chieftains in the west, still beyond significant Norman influence, were building strong stone edifices. These new castles were typically rectangular rather than circular, with high curtain walls to ward off attackers. We can see in the ruins of Tioram a simple rectangle of thick walls (the tower is of later date), with a small entrance. At the top of the wall, in the battlements above the gate is a small projecting machicolation, from which missiles could be dropped onto attackers. Post holes high in the walls show that a wooden walkway would have been mounted on beams set in the walls just below the level of the battlements. Around

Castle Tioram was the power-base of the Lords of the Isles and subsequently of the Macdonalds of Clanranald. It was burned in 1715.

the 1200s some castles began adding round towers high on the corners of the main structure, with arrow slits, and stone keeps began to rise up within defensive curtain walls. We are probably looking at simple rectangular structures, two or three storeys high, with a first floor (American – second-floor) entrance reached by an external stairway giving access to the main hall. There may have been smaller castles at the time but only the remains of the very strongest survive.

The Norman aristocrats were meanwhile beginning to put up similar stone castles, a fine example being Rothesay, built by the Stewarts around 1200, with a massive curtain wall with round towers at the corners. These towers show a distinctly French influence and will not only have improved defences but also provided more living space. Arguably it was the relative peace prevailing in central and southern Scotland in the 13th century that allowed the nobles to build these large castles: they were able to create wealth (not having to finance wars) and had long periods of time un-distracted by fighting – in which to engage in long-term building projects. It should not be forgotten that these were not barracks, but homes for the baronial households, for the family, their employees and their fighting men, and a large castle may easily have had to house 100 – 150 people within its walls, though little of the domestic accommodation is evident in what survives today.

In 1296 a long period of relative peace came to an end when Edward I stormed Berwick and butchered most of its inhabitants. From this time on Scotland found itself at war with the English for some 50 years, then fairly regularly over subsequent centuries. The existing castles did not prove themselves well: all of the great strongholds – Berwick, Roxburgh, Jedburgh, Edinburgh, Stirling – fell relatively easily to the English, were won back again by the Scots, and so on until many of them were destroyed or damaged by Robert the Bruce to prevent their being used again by the English. What castle-builders learned from these experiences was the importance of improved wall-heads, gateways and outer wall defences.

This first series of Wars of Independence ended in 1357 with the return to the throne of David II. Beneficiaries of his return were the families who had stayed loyal, such as the Stewarts, Campbells and Douglasses, whereas the Comyns and other supporters of the English were rapidly to lose their influence in Scotland. Until the turn of the 13th and 14th century the Comyns had been the most powerful clan in Scotland, with good claim to the crown. Their misfortune was to come up against Robert the Bruce who finally secured the throne after defeating his former ally, John Comyn, at the battle of Inverurie, in 1308. Later known as Cumming, they remained a respectable-sized clan, but lost most of their power and many of their estates and castles (including Inverlochie, Balvenie, Urquhart, Blair and more), withdrawing to their clan headquarters at Altyre, Moray.

With the exception of Tantallon, the last great curtain-walled castle, built by the Earl Douglas in the 1360s, the fashion now shifted to smaller tower-houses with outbuildings sheltered within more modest, lower perimeter walls (most of which, together with the outbuildings, do not survive), suggesting that those building these castles were becoming less concerned with defence than their predecessors. The

Caerlaverock was built in the late 13th century to control the south-west border between England and Scotland.

This ruin on Loch an Eilen was once a stronghold of the powerful Comyns family, who fell from grace by unsuccesfully opposing Robert the Bruce.

growing stratum of wealthy Scottish landowners built these tower-houses or hall-houses of a relatively domestic style, with a grand hall, internal staircases, kitchens and latrines, though still with an eye to defence: there were no banks in Scotland yet! Most doorways at this time had two barriers, a wooden door and an iron *yett* - a sort of open-barred gate. Wall-heads were also fortified with projecting corbels, parapets and later on, gun-holes. Starting as simple rectangular towers this style evolved over the next two hundred years into a wide variety of shapes. The first variation was the addition of a wing to produce an L-plan or a T-plan, two to give an E-plan (without the middle bit...), or the larger Z-plan.

After James IV's defeat at Flodden in 1513 Scotland was back into 30 years of war with the English, this time with widespread use of artillery. The latter half of the 15th century had brought a new challenge – the first use of cannon in warfare. Early cannon were inaccurate but bombarded the enemy with immensely heavy stones and castles had to be strengthened to withstand this. Massive defences were built at Dundar, Craignethan (Lanarkshire), Blackness near Edinburgh, and elsewhere and the English began to imitate the Italians by building earthen defensive walls around the bases of the castles they captured. These were better able to absorb the impact of cannon-fire. From the 1560s, despite the departure of the English once again, most new castles incorporated gun-holes in their walls. This period, post-Reformation, represented a time of great change in Scottish society, with wealth and political influence permeating downwards to a new level in society. This led in turn to a noticeable increase in the building of more modest-sized tower-houses at a time when the English upper classes were building stately homes with no military characteristics whatsoever. Life on the Borders remained difficult, with law and order noticeable by its absence and the constant threat of cattle-raiders (*reivers*) and fighting between feuding neighbours, so good fortification was still a necessity here, as it was in other outlying parts of the kingdom.

Castles had also always been built to defend trade routes over land and water. Remote buildings such as Duart and Tioram in the Highlands will have had no function in the Wars of Independence but will have had great strategic importance in terms of controlling local trade and agriculture. Other castles were simply fortified country houses, with no military or political function, or places where the local knight or laird could manage his estates and maintain the social order of things. Urquhart castle, started during the time of the wars in the early 16th century, reminds us that life for many in Scotland remained relatively calm and that most of the people were untouched by fighting on the borders or the coasts. The charter granted to the builder of Urquhart makes it clear that this is really just a fortified country house. By the 17th century the wealthy families were able to build grand mansions such as Thirlestane and Drumlanrig, which made no pretence of any military or defensive function: they simply made a very clear statement about the owners' wealth and prestige. Thirlstane was an important ambassadorial residence but Craigievar in Aberdeenshire is just a soaring monument to the commercial prowess of its owner Willie Forbes, a successful 17th century import/export merchant.

Glencassley is typical of the more modest-sized Highlands sporting estate prized by the Victorians

The 18th and 19th centuries saw the spread of the Scottish Baronial style, with turrets and conical roofs being added to plainer buildings to produce the style considered uniquely Scottish to this day. Finally in the mid-1800s Queen Victoria bought Balmoral and fashionable English and Scots suddenly needed a castle too. Typical of such a "new" estate is Glencassley. Prior to 1870 it was part of the Rosehall estate in Sutherland, bought and broken up by speculators wanting to cash in on the new demand for Scottish sporting (ie – stalking, shooting and fishing) estates. The 9-bedroomed castle dates from the 1870s and was built by the English brewer Charles Flower, founder of The Royal Shakespeare Company. The drawing room is still decorated with scenes from Macbeth, painted by scenery-painters from the theatre in Stratford-on-Avon. This type of sporting property went in and out of fashion over subsequent decades but with modern communications available even this far north, the future popularity of such remote country houses seems guaranteed.

A word from the photographer and the author

There are many, many castles in Scotland. This book is not meant as a comprehensive guide: it is a collection of photographs of some favourites together with a brief introduction to Scotland's history and the place of the castle within that colourful story.

The Borders

The Border referred to is, of course, the border with England's most northerly counties, Northumberland and Cumbria. The region, just an hour or so south of Glasgow and Edinburgh formerly comprised the old counties of Berwickshire, Selkirkshire, Roxburghshire and Peeblesshire and the River Tweed flowing eastwards from its source west of Peebles to join the North Sea at Berwick-upon-Tweed, formed a natural border with England, although for most of its length it runs some miles north of the present-day boundary.

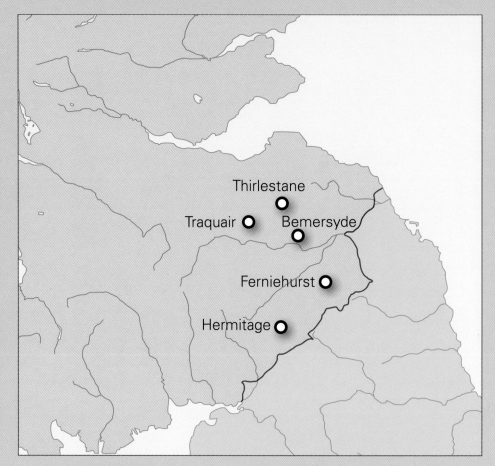

There has been human settlement in the Borders for over 5,000 years, archeological evidence suggesting that it was hunted over at an even earlier period. The Romans, who tended to be shy of straying too far into Scotland arrived in 80 AD to complete the building of their great military road from Dover to Aberdeen. This linked a chain of forts of which Trimontium, at Newstead, three kilometres east of Melrose, was the most important in the 90-mile road-length between the Rivers Tyne and Forth. In 122 AD the new emperor Hadrian visited and decided that a defensive wall should be built running more than 70 miles from the mouth of the River Tyne across to Carlisle and down to the Cumbrian coastline. Hadrian's Wall inadvertently gave birth to the notion of distinct north and south regions of Britain, and many centuries later, the creation of the separate nation of Scotland. The inhabitants of this region were always closely linked through landscape, sheep farming, history and culture to Northumbria to the south and up until the 9th century this region of what could then be thought of as *mid-Britain* flourished and prospered. One Roman commentator, however, declared that the Britons could not be kept under Roman control and described this northern region as 'Britannica Barbarica', a place of hostile tribes, and the occupiers finally departed behind the protection of Hadrian's Wall in 180 AD.

During the medieval period great monasteries and abbeys were built in Kelso, Jedburgh, Melrose and Dryburgh. The wealthy wool traders chose to export from Berwick direct to Europe rather than to their southern neighbours. Writers, scholars and intellectuals too travelled to share and exchange ideas and culture throughout civilised Europe. This golden age was however to come to an end with the death of Alexander III in 1286. The Wars of Independence between England and Scotland began, seriously affecting the Border territory with brutal warfare and widespread destruction. Law and order broke down and the Border *reivers* began to harry the landowners and farmers, plundering everything they could find. The English and the Scots, until then relatively close and friendly neighbours, began to steal cattle, sheep and horses from each other, like some wild west rustlers in the America of the 19th century. Like the wild west, much of this brutality has been glamorised in the literature of the Borders, with Walter Scott perhaps the best known chronicler of the region.

The hardship of these times was exacerbated by the constant fighting with the English for control of the region, fighting which did not finally end until the mid-18th century. Berwick, situated in the vitally important defensive position at the mouth of the Tweed, changed hands between England and Scotland thirteen times between the 12th and 15th centuries. Berwick is now just south of the border but very Scottish in character.

Since the start of the Iron Age, some 600 years before the arrival of the Romans, the locals had built fortified settlements. The use of these communal sites declined as forests were cleared and agriculture spread and living in individual houses dotted over a wider area became more convenient. The Danes invaded the area in 886, the next serious invasion, with lasting consequences, being that of the Normans in 1072.

The Borders has, not surprisingly, a large number of castles in addition to its famous abbeys: these include Hermitage, Bemersyde, Ferniehurst, Traquair and Thirlestane (all photographed and described on the following pages), Aikwood Tower (recently restored by Lord Steel of Aikwood, former leader of the Liberal party), Smailholm Tower (the setting for Walter Scott's *Marmion*), Floors (the largest inhabited mansion in Scotland and home to the Dukes of Roxburghe), Neidpath Castle, and Borthwick, the tallest tower house in Scotland.

Hermitage

Standing between Hawick and Newcastleton, the gloomy, almost malevolent pile of Hermitage dominates Liddesdale, known as "the bloodiest valley in Britain". Sir Walter Scott wrote of it:

"The Castle... unable to support the load of iniquity which had long been accumulating within its walls, is supposed to have partly sunk beneath the ground; and its ruins are still regarded by the peasants with peculiar aversion and horror."

In 1242, according to John de Fordun, England and Scotland came to the brink of war because of the building of Hermitage, Henry III objecting that it was too close to the border, which was then the river Liddle. This would have been an early wooden structure, not the stone pile seen here. The later stone castle was built around 1350 and, unashamedly a defensive structure, consisted of a rectangular courtyard surrounded by living quarters.

The first castle on this site was built in 1242 by the Norman Sir Nicholas de Soulis, at that time butler to the king. His son, William, was boiled alive in a cauldron by his own servants, after hearing a prophesy that he could never be harmed by steel nor bound by rope – which he thought meant he was invincible.

On a circle of stone they placed the pot,
On a circle of stones but barely nine,
They heated it up red and fiery hot,
Till the burnished brass did glimmer and shine.

They rolled him up in a sheet of lead,
A sheet of lead for a funeral pall,
They plunged him in the cauldron red.
and melted him lead bones and all.

(The Boiling of Bad Lord Soulis)

The castle passed back and forth between the Scots and the English. Hermitage was frequently mentioned during the Wars of Independence and in 1300 Edward I ordered its repair at a cost of 20 pounds. In 1320 the de Soulis family forfeited the estate to the crown when William de Soulis was accused of attempting to kill the then king Robert the Bruce. By 1332, when Edward Balliol seized the Scottish throne back from the Bruces, Hermitage was once more in English hands. In the late 1330s ownership passed to William Douglas, knight of Liddesdale. He was feared and respected in Scotland on account of his victories against the English, but when King David II made Sir Alexander Ramsay sheriff of Teviotdale, Douglas was furious. Believing that the position should be his own he lured the unfortunate Ramsay to Hermitage and imprisoned him in a "frightful pit or Dungeon, apparently airless and devoid of sanitation". The sherriff was starved to death, and his ghostly groans have been heard by visitors to Hermitage ever since. From Douglas the castle passed to Hugh de Dacre, the first owner to reconstruct the buildings

It is not known where the name Hermitage derives from. Before it was built the area may have been the retreat of a holy man.

wholly of stone. Towards the end of the century, after a brief spell in the hands of the English, Hermitage was given to the Douglases, one of the most powerful Borders families, and the oldest parts of the present stone structure date from this period. It was designed so that wooden fighting platforms could be run along the whole length of the outside of the tops of the walls and in 1390 the third Earl Douglas further improved the castle's defences by the addition of the massive stone towers at each corner. Later the castle was granted to the Hepburns, Earls of Bothwell after one of the Douglases showed himself rather too supportive of the English. Mary Queen of Scots famously rode 50 miles in one day, from and back to Jedburgh, to be at James Hepburn, 4th Earl of Bothwell's side when he sustained a serious injury in 1566. Hermitage finally passed into the hands of that other great Border family, the Scotts of Buccleuch in the 17th century. Within one hundred years its value as a defensive castle had gone and it was abandoned, to be restored in the 18th century when Walter Scott's writings about various of the castle legends revived interest in Hermitage.

Another legend concerns a mound near the ruined chapel a quarter-mile north-west of the castle. It is said to be the grave of a giant called the Cout o' Keilder, who terrorised the area, and wore magical chain mail which could protect him from all blows. He was, however, finally defeated and killed by drowning in a deep pool of water in the river known as the drowning pool.

Bemersyde

Bemersyde, 1¼ miles (2 km) north-east of Newtown St. Boswells and close to the River Tweed, has been home to the Haig family – famed as much for the eponymous whisky as for the WWI general, Field Marshal Sir Douglas (later, Earl) Haig – since their arrival from Normandy in the 1130s. Although the present lofty tower-house, sited high above the banks of the Tweed seems typically 16th century there are some walls over ten feet thick, clearly pointing to much earlier origins. It was here that the soothsayer and poet, Thomas the Rhymer, prophesied:

Time and tide, what may betide
There'll aye be Haigs at Bemersyde

Thomas of Ercildoune lived in the Scottish Borders near the Eildon Hills in the 14th century and in these hills he met the Fairy Queen who made him to go to Fairyland for three years. On his return he had the gift of prophecy and usually made his pronouncements in rhyme – hence his soubriquet, Thomas the Rhymer. His prediction about the Haigs looked like being proved wrong when the family line died out in the 19th century, but in 1921 the castle was restored to the then Earl Haig as a gift from the nation for his services in WWI, and is owned by his family to this day.

The oldest part of the present house, the central portion, dates from the 1500s, with the top storey built around a hundred years later. The east and west extensions are later additions. The original stronghold would have been enclosed within a pale, or curtain-wall.

The castle was repaired in the late 1500s, having been seriously damaged by the English during The Rough Wooing in the 1540s.

There is a curse on the statue of the outlaw, Wattie Elliott, that anyone who moves him will die.

The old tower was built in 1535 and a further storey added during the renovations of 1585.
The two wings were added in the 18th century.

Field Marshal Haig was commander-in-chief of the British forces in France during World War I. His study contains a wealth of memorabilia, including signed photographs of many of the allied leaders.

The huge thickness of the walls gives some indication of the age of the castle.
This room has always been the bedroom or private quarters of the Laird.

Ferniehurst

Ferniehurst (or –hirst) castle stands about 1.5 miles south of Jedburgh, on a minor road east of the A68, and east of the Jed Water. This L-shaped Borders stronghold, or fortalice, was built by the Kerr family in 1476 on the remains of an earlier structure. The castle has had a lively military history, being sacked by the English in 1523, re-taken with French help in 1549 and used by Sir Thomas Kerr, protector of Mary Queen of Scots, to invade England in 1570, in a vain attempt to rescue her. Retaliation followed and James VI destroyed the castle in 1593. It was rebuilt about 1598 but began its decline into dilapidation around 200 years ago. Used latterly as a wartime army billet, then a youth hostel, it has been restored by its present occupant, Lord Lothian, who lives in a new wing, built on older foundations. The tower boasts a number of romantic conically-capped corner turrets, known as studies, which open from the rooms of the upper floor and are decorative rather than defensive – true baronial style!

When Lord Lothian is in residence his flag flies from the tower.

The circular library, off the great hall.

A detail of the chapel door, built in 1622 by Sir Andrew Kerr.

The Red Boy is Sir Robert Kerr, who bankrupted the estate in the 17th century.

The staircase is said to have been specially designed for the left-handed Kerr family.

Thirlestane

Thirlestane is one of the finest and most impressive 17th century palaces to be seen anywhere in Europe. The re-construction began in 1670 for the 2nd Earl and Duke of Thirlestane (John Maitland), who was Lord Chancellor of Scotland for Charles II. It was designed to impress, both in its size and architectural detail, inside and out. It is built of red sandstone and stands on the site of the original Lauder Fort, a wooden structure used by Edward I as a military base for the 1296 invasion of Scotland. The location dominated the main road to Edinburgh, hence its military significance over subsequent centuries.

A stone castle replaced the fort around 1400 and ownership passed back and forth between England and Scotland, settling with the Maitlands of Thirlestane, who continued to strengthen the fort's defences into the late 1500s and maintained the fabric of the castle long after its political significance had declined, making further substantial improvements as late as 1840, when the two large wings were added.

The towers were added in the 1670s, 100 years after the building of the keep.

Next page: Thirlestane is a real fairy-tale castle with a splendid display of turrets and pointed roofs, all designed to be seen and admired from far away.

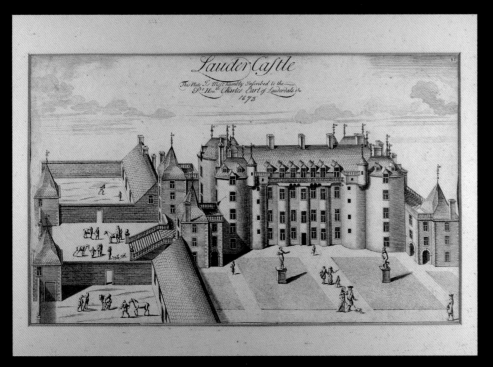

The Duke of Lauderdale remodelled Thirlestane (then known as Lauder) as shown in this 1670s print.

Carefully-worked pink sandstone contrasts with the rough local stone of the walls.

Traquair

Traquair is the home of one of Scotland's most famous families, the Stuarts. It, like one or two other castles, lays claim to being the oldest continuously inhabited house in Scotland. The Quair burn joins the River Tweed a few hundred yards from the rear of the house and *tre* was a Gaelic word for house or hamlet. No-one knows when the first building was put up here in the middle of the great Ettrick forest, but Traquair was in use as a hunting lodge for Alexander I by 1107. By the end of the 13th century it was playing its part among the string of defensive forts along the Tweed and the border with England. When the alarm was raised they could communicate with each other by lighting a beacon at the top of the tower to alert the neighbours of an English invasion. Traquair was occupied by both Edward I and II during the Wars of Independence but taken back by Robert the Bruce after Bannockburn in 1314. James Stuart, first Laird of Traquair, was given the house by his father, the Earl of Buchan in 1491, after he had somehow persuaded the then owner to part with it for the sum of £3.75p (US$7.50)! The 7th Laird, a supporter of Charles I, was made Earl of Traquair but over the following decades the family fell from favour, adopting Catholicism and supporting the Jacobites, so that by the end of the 18th century the family fortunes were at a very low ebb, with substantial debts. The earldom lapsed in 1861 and the castle passed to another branch of the family, the Maxwell-Stuarts.

During the 16th century the main building was extended so by 1599 the main body of the house was completed. Then in the early 1600s the 7th Laird added the top storey, realigned the windows and changed the course of the River Tweed so it ran further away from the house. Little building work was done to the castle after 1695, when the Edinburgh architect James Smith added the two side wings and the double terrace, pavilions and formal gardens at the back of the house, other than the conversion of part of the ground floor into a Catholic chapel, in 1829.

Overleaf: The Stuarts lost most of their influence and wealth after 1745 with the consequence that little work was done to Traquair. As a result it looks much the same today as it did 300 years ago.

Legend has it that these gates were last opened for Bonnie Prince Charlie in 1745.

A bell in the servants' quarters.

The 17th century staircase.

This is said to be the bed in which Mary Queen of Scots spent her last night in Scotland.

Central Region

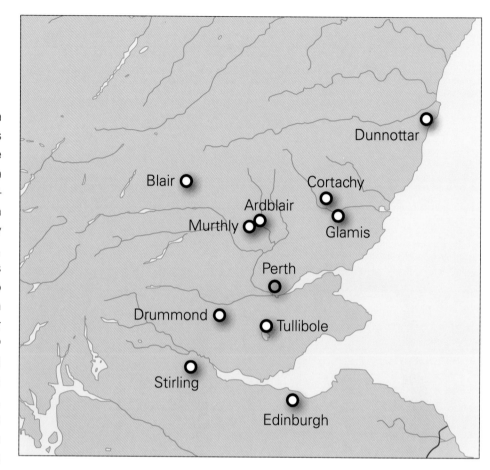

The area covered in this chapter extends from the edge of the Borders in the south to the Grampians in the north and incorporates the ancient Pictish region of Angus (from King Oengus), Glasgow and Edinburgh. The first settlers in the region are generally referred to as the Picts, from the Latin name *picti* (painted people) given by the Roman Eumenius in 297 AD. It is possible that they were Iberian hunter-gatherers who reached Scotland around 7000 BC, via France and southern Britain (England). One of their rare remaining campsites is at Morton in Fife. They probably developed a Neolithic farming life over the period of about 4,000 – 2,000 BC, seeing the introduction of tools and pottery and the development of communities and early religious activity. They were almost certainly of a different ethnic group to the Celts, who were also colonising the region at the time. When St. Columba, a Celt, came over from Ireland in 565 AD it is reported that he needed an interpreter when he preached to the Pictish King Brudei on the banks of Loch Ness. By the 6th century King Fergus and his Scots (ie – Irish!) had invaded Argyll and established the realm of Dalriada and the Picts appear to have been driven into the northern and east-central regions. A hundred years later, after the departure of the Romans, the Scots and Picts united to attempt to fight off the aggressive Angles and Saxons of Northumbria, culminating in victory at the Battle of Dunnichen, near Forfar, in the 7th century. This decisive victory ended the Northumbrian attempts at domination of the Picts, curbing their expansion northwards, and created the foundations for the Scotland we know today. Over a century after the battle the Northumbrian historian, Bede, wrote an account of it:

"Egfrith, King of Northumbria, rashly led an army to ravage the province of the Picts. The enemy pretended to retreat, and lured the king into narrow mountain passes, where he was killed with the greater part of his forces.... Many of the English at this time were killed, or forced to flee from Pictish territory."

Fighting between Picts and Scots was fairly constant until the arrival of a new enemy, the Norseman, in the 9th century, and by 842, Kenneth Mac Alpin, King of Dalriada had decided to move his court to the relative safety of Scone, not far from Perth. The depredations of the Norsemen to the west and in the Isles led eventually to the building of the earliest stone defensive castles still surviving today. Edinburgh (Dun Eideann) did not replace Scone as capital of Scotland until 1437 but both Stirling and Edinburgh were clearly critically important sites as early as the end of the first millennium and the whole region grew in political and economic importance from this time on as attention gradually shifted to the common enemy in the south.

Glasgow was founded by the early missionary, St. Mungo, and became first and foremost a religious centre. The industrial revolution brought its significant economic growth many ceturies later. A castle known as Bishop's Castle did, until the late 18th century, stand on the site since occupied by Glasgow's Royal Infirmary. It was originally a royal fortress, becoming home to the bishops of Glasgow by the end of the 13th century, when William Wallace and his 300 men defeated an army of 1,000 English knights who had occupied the castle under the instructions of the bishop of Durham. Two centuries later this castle was again the scene of battle when opposing forces fought for control of the crown of Scotland then in the possession of the infant Mary Queen of Scots. The only other major medieval building in the city of Glasgow is the cathedral.

To the north Perth stands on the banks of the river Tay. The name is Pictish and the town is just two miles from Scone, the royal heart of *Alba* from the mid-9th century. King David granted the town *burgh* status in the early 12th century and it developed into a wealthy international trading community. Perth's royal castle was destroyed by a flood as long ago as 1209, and a car-park now stands on the site… The 14th century Scottish civil wars can be said to have started in Perth when Edward III's pretender, Balliol, invaded at Perth to seize the crown in 1332, three years after the death of Robert the Bruce. Edward III subsequently built massive defensive walls so that Perth became the best-defended town in Scotland during the middle ages. The last evidence of these structures was demolished around 1810.

Glamis Castle

Most of us are familiar with the name of Glamis Castle from Shakespeare's *Macbeth*, although the events he describes as taking place here would have occurred almost 400 years before the castle was actually built. Set spectacularly among the rolling Angus hills this huge building, a riot of towers and turrets, is reached via an avenue a good mile long. Glamis was the childhood home of Elizabeth Bowes-Lyon, the late Queen Mother, and birthplace of Queen Elizabeth II and her late sister, Princess Margaret.

Its links with royalty are strong. As far back as 700 AD, when Glamis was a shrine to St. Fergus, the surrounding area was a hunting ground for the kings of Alba. We know that it was still hunted 300 years later as in 1034 King Malcolm died, probably of wounds sustained at the Battle of Hunters Hill, and was brought from the battle to the royal hunting lodge which stood on this site (though it is also said that he was murdered here).

The Lyon (now Bowes-Lyon) family's first connection with Glamis came in 1372 when Sir John Lyon of Forteviot became Thane of Glamis and was given the royal hunting lodge, for services rendered to the king, Robert II – and for marrying his daughter. Sir John's son also married a Stewart princess and started the construction of the castle in 1404, building what is today the east wing, but would originally have been a simple, free-standing, fortified tower. His son extended the building with an L-shaped keep with a massive great hall. Over the centuries the family fortunes rose and fell. In 1537 James V took the castle and lands and stole most of the valuable contents, Mary Queen of Scots restoring the estates to the family some 25 years later. Over the following hundred years Glamis was extended more as a comfortable baronial country house than as a military stronghold, as the outer defensive walls made way for formal gardens. By the mid-18th century it was the marriage of John Lyon – then the 9th Earl of Strathmore and Kinghorne, Viscount Lyon and Baron of Glamis – to the fabulously wealthy Mary Eleanor Bowes that saved the family from crippling debts.

Glamis is reputed to have more ghosts than any other Scottish castle. The Grey Lady is Janet Douglas, widow of the 6th Earl, who was falsely accused of witchcraft and plotting to poison the king, imprisoned and burned at the stake. She now haunts the area around the clock tower and her ghost can sometimes be seen in the chapel sitting on a pew at the back of the building, or praying at the altar. She is not to be confused with The White Lady who also haunts the castle grounds, though nothing more is known about her story. A young black boy – Britain's only black ghost? – a servant in the 18th century who was mistreated by his masters, can sometimes be seen on the stone seat outside the Queen's bedroom. Alexander Earl Crawford (also known as Beardie) lost his soul to the devil in a card game and is said to be locked in a secret room in the castle, playing cards for all eternity. Look out also for the distraught ghost of an unknown woman with no tongue leaning out of a window or running through the castle grounds pointing at her mutilated face…

Glamis started life as a 15th century hunting lodge.

Photos of the Queen and the late Queen mother, whose home was Glamis.

A collection of coats of arms featured on the courtyard walls.

Built in the early 1600s, this staircase gave access to all parts of the building from the front door – for the first time.

Originally a simple fortified keep, Glamis castle is now a huge complex bristling with towers, turrets and conical roofs.

As may be expected Glamis boasts art, furniture, and artifacts from all over the world.

The 15th century kitchens with their huge fireplace are situated below the original great hall of the castle.

Edinburgh

Little of Edinburgh's castle pre-dates the 16th century, except for St Margaret's Chapel, the oldest surviving building in the city: it is early 12th century. There does however seem to have been significant activity here since Roman times. In the latter half of the 11th century: John of Fordun's account of the death of King Malcolm III places his widow, the future Saint Margaret, at the "Castle of Maidens" (which is Edinburgh) when she learns of his death in 1093 and the first meeting of the Scottish Parliament occurred at the castle around 1140. When Edward I invaded Scotland in 1296 he besieged and captured Edinburgh Castle. In 1314, Robert the Bruce's nephew, Sir Thomas Randolph, led his men up the steep north face of Edinburgh Castle rock, took the English garrison by surprise and won the castle back. Robert the Bruce immediately ordered that Edinburgh castle be dismantled "lest the English ever afterwards might lord it over the land by holding the castles". The governor of Edinburgh Castle at the time of the Glorious Revolution was the Duke of Gordon, a Jacobite, and his resistance to the arrival of William of Orange led to a siege of Edinburgh castle, beginning in March 1689 and lasting for three months, during which time William and Mary were finally offered, and accepted the Scottish Crown. On 13 June Gordon surrendered. This was the last serious military action seen by Edinburgh castle. The great hall with its splendid hammer beam roof was built in 1511 on the orders of King James IV and the crown room holds *the honours of Scotland*, the crown jewels.

The site of Edinburgh Castle has obvious strategic importance.

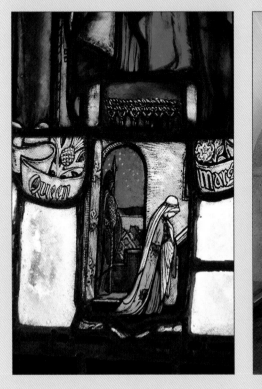

St. Margaret's Chapel, built in the early 1100s, is Edinburgh's oldest building.

The castle, from Calton Hill, with the Balmoral Hotel clock in the foreground.

Little of the castle's present structure is earlier than the 16th century, the great hall being built by James IV in 1511.

Stirling Castle, the gateway to the central region, has been attacked or besieged at least 16 times.

Stirling

The other significant royal castle in the region is Stirling; guarding the lowest crossing point of the River Forth, this would have been of strategic importance to anyone wanting to control central Scotland and, as proof of this, it has been attacked or besieged at least 16 times. With the exception of the 18th century outer defences, most of the surviving buildings of Stirling Castle date back to the period from 1496 to 1583, the time of James IV, V and VI. But, along with other royal castles, Stirling did provide a home for the peripatetic Scottish kings and queens from the days of Alexander I, who died here in 1124. The first "modern" stone castle was built here around 1280 but none of these buildings remain. It was the last Scottish castle to surrender to Edward I, in 1304, but after returning to Scots hands after Bannockburn it was, like many another Scottish castle, destroyed to keep it out of the control of future English invaders. Despite this ownership passed back and forth between the English and the Scots until James IV, fresh from murdering his father at Sauchieburn in 1488, began the extensive rebuilding which to a great extent survives today. Mary Queen of Scots, not yet one year old, was crowned here in 1543. She had become queen at the age of six days, on the death of her father, aged 30.

The British army used the castle as a barracks for over 150 years, finally moving out in 1964. It remains the official headquarters of the Argyll and Sutherland Highlanders, and houses their regimental museum.

The thickness of the walls indicates the age of the Great Hall.

The Great Hall, with its magnificent oak beams and stained glass windows, is medieval but was restored and re-opened in 1999.

The freshness and brightness of the colours caused controversy when the newly-restored Great Hall was opened in 1999.

The magnificent hilltop position meant that attackers could never rely on surprising the defenders of Stirling Castle.

James V completed the building of Stirling Palace around 1540. He wanted to demonstrate that Scotland could match the best of contemporary French architecture.

Ardblair

Blairgowrie in Perthshire boasts two castles, both still occupied, and sharing a ghost. Newton Castle is now the home of the Chief of the Clan Macpherson, but it was originally a Drummond stronghold, built in the middle of the 16th century. *Ardblair* Castle built by Alexander de Blair, is considerably older. The estate of Ardblair was granted to Thomas Blair by Robert III in 1399 but the current L-shaped tower was built by his descendants around 1540, and is the oldest remaining part of the castle. The castle is still lived in and the surrounding area farmed by descendants of the daughter of James Blair, the latter having died without a male heir in the mid-1700s. The gaelic word *ard* means "spit of land" or "promontory", which indicates that the original castle was surrounded on three sides by the waters of the loch. *Blair* often indicates the site of a battle (from the Celtic word for a clearing, a logical place to have a battle…) all of which suggests that Ardblair was at one time a strategically important military or defensive site. In the mid-16th century two members of the neighbouring Drummond family were murdered by the Blairs. At the time, Lady Jean Drummond was in love with one of the Blair sons. Clearly her family were now not prepared to sanction a match, and neither were the Blairs, as Patrick Blair had been beheaded for his part in the murder. Heartbroken, Lady Jean left the shelter of her castle and was never seen again. Her ghost, however, dressed in green silk and known as The Green Lady, divides her time between the two castles.

The statue depicts Persephone, queen of the underworld.

Tregoid Taurus, the last Hereford bull bought by the estate.

A view from within the courtyard showing the 16th century towerhouse on original 12th century foundations.

The oldest part of the present structure at Ardblair dates back to 1540, but it stands on the foundations of an ancient Pictish fortress.

Queen Victoria may well have sat in this 18th century drawing room when she visited Blair in 1844.

Blair Castle

Blair Castle, set on a key strategic route to the Highlands, is the ancient seat of the Earls of Atholl. Built at the foot of the Grampian mountains, on the route to Inverness, this castle's history stretches back at least 750 years to 1269. At that time the Earl of Atholl was David Strathbogie. He had been on a crusade and on his return discovered that one John Comyn had built a tower on his land. This tower stands to this day, known as Cumming's Tower, and is the oldest part of Blair Castle. Over the centuries Blair found itself at the heart of many of the intrigues and the battles caused by the hostilities between England and Scotland and, particularly, the Wars of Religion in the 17th century. Cromwell occupied Blair from 1652 until 1660. The Atholls fiercely resisted the Union with England at the beginning of the 18th century with the result that the then Duke was placed under house arrest for several years. Later that century the family's loyalties became divided over the Jacobite cause and Blair became the last place in Britain to be besieged, during the last Jacobite rising. Bonnie Prince Charlie had stayed at the castle on his way south in that year. Perhaps as a direct result of this it was occupied in 1746 by Hanoverian troops and then besieged by Jacobite forces on their way to Culloden.

The castle remained in the hands of the Dukes and Earls of Atholl but the title changed hands several times before being granted to the Murray family by Charles I in 1629. They have retained ownership since then. Through the years of military turmoil the castle was damaged and repaired several times but was comprehensively remodelled in the mid-1700s, when many of the military-looking features, such as the crenellations, were removed, and again in the mid-19th century. This latter redesign followed a visit of Queen Victoria in 1844, who described Blair as "a large, plain, white building". So the medieval towers and crenellations were restored, to make it look more like a "castle". The queen was, however, so impressed by her guard of a hundred Atholl Highlanders that she presented them with regimental colours, and they are now the only private army permitted in Europe.

In the 1860s the towers and crenellations, removed in 1740, were restored in the Scottish baronial style, and a new entrance was built.

Bonnie Prince Charlie slept in the Tullibardine Room in 1745.

The highest part of Blair, Cumming's Tower, was built in 1269.

A selection of typical 17th century Scottish oak chairs, in a style known as *caqueteuse*, from the French word for a *gossip*.

Blair's position, at the gateway to the Highlands, is strategically important.

Cortachy

Cortachy Castle, a massive whitewashed baronial pile, is built on the banks of the river South Esk, strategically placed to guard the entrance to Glen Cova and overlooking the valley of Strathmore. A castle was first built on this site in 1330 by the Stewart Earls of Strathearn, though the Ogilvie family had been granted the Barony and the estate as early as 1163. The Ogilvies were staunch Royalists and many held high offices of state. In 1491 Sir James Ogilvie was rewarded with the title Lord Ogilvie of Airlie, with the 8th Lord receiving an Earldom from Charles I. A direct consequence of these Royalist sympathies and the Airlies' refusal to sign the National Covenant, intended to strengthen and preserve the separation of the Scottish and English churches, was the destruction of the family's prime residence, Airlie Castle, by the Earl of Argyle in 1641.

Argyle he has ta'en five hunder o'his Men,
Five hunder men and mairly,
And he's awa by yon green shaw
Come to plunder the Bonnie Hoose O' Airlie.

Clouds o'smoke and flames sae high
Sune left the wa's but barely,
And she laid doon on that hill to dee,
When she saw the burnin' o'Airlie.

Following this the family seat was moved to Cortachy, which they had been given by James III in 1473, and where they remain in residence to this day. The Ogilvies continued their support for the Stuart cause for the next century, culminating in the provision of an Angus regiment led by the 5th Earl at Culloden. Following his defeat at the battle, the Earl went into exile in France and forfeited the title, which was finally restored to the family in 1826.

Robert the Bruce is said to have had a hunting lodge here, which suggests that the building of the first castle was perhaps associated with the freeing up of the estate following his death in 1329. The present structure is based upon a Z-plan form and was built in the mid-1400s but rebuilt in the 16th century and much altered over subsequent years. The main rebuilding took place in 1871 when the architect David Bryce remodelled the castle in the then popular Scottish Baronial style, adding battlements and the "typically Scottish" conical roofs to the towers. The work cost a staggering £30,000! The oldest part of the castle, the south wing, dates from the 16th century. Three original round towers, one with a rectangular watch-room at the top, corbelled-out on a W-shaped support can also still be seen today.

Originally the great hall, this drawing room was remodelled in 1871 with a copy of a Jacobean ceiling and a minstrel's gallery.

The oldest parts of Cortachy date from the mid-1500s but it was remodelled in the 19th century in the Scottish Baronial style.
The first castle on the site was built in 1330 by the Stewart Earl of Strathearn.

The grave of David, 9th Earl of Airlie, killed in action in the Boer War in 1900.

A portrait of the 12th Laird Ogilvie.

Cortachy has been home to the Earls of Airlie since 1641.

A portrait of Charles II by Mary Beale (1633 -1699).

Charles II stayed in this room for one night in 1650.

The splendid formal gardens date to at least 1630, when the idiosyncratic sundial was erected. Unlike the castle itself, the gardens remain open to the public.

Drummond

In 1314 Sir Malcolm Drummond fought for Robert the Bruce at Bannockburn and was rewarded with the grant of land at Strathearn. Drummond castle was built here in 1491 by his descendant, Sir John Drummond. The Drummonds have had as colourful a history as any of the warlike clans of Scotland. In the 14th century Scottish foot-soldiers, armed with spears, swords and shields were generally no match for the armoured, mounted cavalry of the English. At Bannockburn Sir Malcolm had his men spread *caltrops* – vicious four-pointed iron stars – under the hooves of the advancing English horses. Once unseated the heavily armoured cavalry were slaughtered by the Scottish infantry. As a reward Drummond was given the right to use the caltrop as a symbol in his coat of arms. When William Drummond, like many another disappointed Royalist, fled the country in the mid-1600s he became an adviser at the court of the Tsar of Russia. There he noted the efficacy of the thumbscrew as an instrument of torture and on his return home had the device introduced to the unfortunate British. Two Drummond women became queens of Scotland, Margaret marrying David II in 1363 and Annabella the future Robert II in 1366. Sir John Drummond's daughter, Margaret, was the lover of James IV of Scotland who some Scottish nobles wished to see married to the sister of Henry VII of England. To ensure that there would be no danger of a marriage to Margaret, they had her and her two sisters murdered by supplying them with poisoned fruit.

The power and wealth of the Drummonds was a direct result of their continuing loyalty to the Scottish throne. In common with other Royalist families, however, they saw their family estates attacked and severely damaged by Cromwellian forces and eventually forfeited after the Jacobite defeat at Culloden. The seat now belongs to the Earls of Ancaster, descended from a female Drummond line to whom the lands were restored in 1784.

The original tower of the castle was rebuilt after the Cromwellian siege but destroyed again after Culloden by the family themselves, so that it could not be used by the Hanoverians. A large Victorian mansion was added in the 19th century, giving the castle its current appearance of two neighbouring houses rather than one unified structure. Its most famous feature is the Italianate garden, laid out in 1630. Much of the statuary was added in the 1800s but the unique sundial dates from the 17th century, and boasts 50 faces giving the time in many different European cities. In the movie "Rob Roy, Legends of the Mist", Drummond Castle and gardens were used for the residence of Montrose.

Following page: The Drummond castle we see today comprises two different groups of buildings, one dating from the 15th – 17th centuries, and one from Victorian times.

The 17th century sundial in the Italian garden has 50 faces showing the time in numerous European cities.

Dunnottar

Yet another of the strongholds battered by Cromwell's cannon, Dunnottar initially fared better than most, withstanding the siege for a full eight months and saving *the honours of Scotland* – the Scottish crown jewels – from the invaders. This castle was the historic home of the Earls Marischal of Scotland, whose functions included court ceremonial, the management of coronations and the protection of the crown jewels. Charles II had fled to Scotland the year after his father's execution and had been crowned Charles II at Scone. Normally the crown jewels would have been returned to Edinburgh castle but it had already been taken by the Cromwellian forces. The jewels were therefore taken to Dunnottar where a tiny force of 70 men held out against the English army for eight months. The jewels were finally lowered out of a seaward window to a waiting servant woman who took them to a nearby church where they were hidden for several years. Cromwell's army would otherwise have destroyed them as they did the English crown jewels.

Spectacularly situated near Stonehaven in The Mearns, 15 miles from Aberdeen, on a plateau surrounded on three sides by the sea, the castle was built around 1390 on the site of a much earlier Pictish stronghold. The cliffs rise over 160 feet (50 metres) from the sea and the site occupies three acres. St Ninian is said to have come to Dunnottar in the late 400s, converting the Picts to Christianity and founding a chapel here. A chronicle from the 7th century, *The Annals of Ulster*, refers to a siege at *duin foither* – Dunnottar. King Donald II was killed here by Viking raiders in 895 and Athelstan of Essex tried and failed to take it in 934.

The builder of the present castle was the Great Marischal Sir William Keith and the family held on to the title and the castle until they forfeited it to the English crown in consequence of their support for the Jacobite uprising of 1715. The buildings were so badly damaged by the English in 1651 and again by the Duke of Argyll following the Earl's conviction for treason, that the castle fell into disrepair and remained unoccupied until the 20th century when it was bought and restored by the Cowdray family. Much of the main tower or keep survives as does the 13th century stone-built chapel - a relic of the time when William Wallace burnt the early wooden castle with the occupying English garrison inside. The castle also boasts a 120-foot (35-metre) long ballroom – one of the biggest in Scotland.

The 14th century tower house on the site of a much earlier Pictish stronghold was seriously damaged by Cromwell's cannons, but after some restoration earlier this century, is still intact. Dunnottar Castle comprises eleven different buildings, including barracks, lodgings, stables and storehouses.

The Stewarts acquired Murthly in 1615 and created this courtyard, though the entrance, with its Venetian window, is an addition from 1790.

Murthly

The 12,000-acre Murthly Estate lies in the heart of Perthshire, a few miles from Dunkeld, sheltered on the west side by Birnam Hill and overlooking the River Tay. At its centre is Murthly Castle, set amongst some of the tallest and oldest trees in Scotland. The castle is still a private home, owned by the same family, descendants of Sir William Stewart who bought the castle in 1615. "Bought" is perhaps too kind a word: at the time Sir William owned the neighbouring estate and Murthly belonged to his cousin, an Abercrombie, from whom Sir William effectively stole it. He accused Abercrombie of illegally hiding Jesuit priests in his house, threatening to denounce him to James VI. Abercrombie let himself be blackmailed and sold Murthly to Stewart for a nominal sum.

The castle had been started in the 15th century, originally as a typical, five-storey, fortified tower. By Sir William's time it had been extended to an L-Plan keep with additional capped turrets and a gabled tower. In the following centuries various extensions were built and some of them burned down and others were demolished. There is also a 17th century chapel dedicated to St Anthony the Eremite, which was refurbished by Pugin (of Palace of Westminster fame) and was the first consecrated catholic church in Scotland since the reformation. Although the estate is not open to the public, the chapel can still be used for weddings.

In the 1820s the 6th Baronet, Sir John Drummond Stewart, had made the grand tour in Europe and built up an impressive collection of art and artifacts. He commissioned an extension and modernization which was planned to make Murthly the largest private house in Scotland. He ran out of money and died before his dream could be realized, leaving the estate to his eccentric younger brother, Sir William "Buffalo" Stewart. After serving under Wellington at Waterloo and becoming a captain in the Hussars, in 1832 he decided to retire from the army and visit America. First travelling to St. Louis, he then made several expeditions to the west, visited Cuba, speculated in cotton and traded furs, and earned his nickname by returning to the castle with a herd of buffalo and a collection of North American trees and plants. Loathing the rest of his family, he left all the contents of the castle to a Texan, Frank Rice Nicholls, thought to be his illegitimate son. Nicholls sold everything, though much has been found and re-purchased by the owners of Murthly during the past hundred or so years.

The tower was built in 1405, on an older structure.

The yew walk is used by the Lairds only to attend their own funerals.

A detail from the pediment above the entrance.

The ballroom was rebuilt after being destroyed by a fire in 1852. A guest, staying there at the time, was woken by his manservant saying "Arise my Lord, the castle is in flames".

Tullibole

Tullibole Castle is a good example of a nobleman's house of the early 17th century, built on the 'palace' plan. Simple in design it was probably built in 1608, the date shown on the marriage stone over the castle's front doorway. However letters of Edward I dating from 1304 mention a castle on this site and it is possible that the work in 1608 was a refurbishment and extension, rather than a completely new building. The evidence for this is that the door is set in a square tower containing a staircase to the upper floors, yet there exist the remains of an intramural staircase built into the thickness of the castle wall itself and this would undoubtedly be of earlier construction.

The castle now belongs to the Moncreiff family who gained it through marriage to the Halliday clan who had owned Tullibole from 1598 until 1722. It is situated between the hunting forests of the Palace of Falkland and Stirling Castle. The grounds include remnants of a medieval church and cemetery with a rare 9th century Gaelic-Norse *hogback* stone (a carved grave-marker in the early Norse tradition).

The marriage stone over the doorway at Tullibole shows the date of 1608, and celebrates the wedding of Sir John and Lady Halliday.

The door half way up the wall on the left shows that this room, the great hall, was once divided over two floors and will have had an intramural staircase.

The stone-built castle of Tullibole was harled (rendered) and whitewashed in the 1950s. The machicolation above the early 17th century door suggests that defence was still a consideration at that time.

The crow-stepped gables and dormer windows were added in the remodelling of 1842

Bamff

The Ramsays, who hold the splendidly Scottish title – The Ramsay of Bamff – were granted the estate in Perthshire by King Alexander II of Scotland in 1232, and still live in Bamff House almost 800 years later – though not in the same building. Nessus de Ramsay had been the king's physician and his descendants are thought to have completed the first castle on the site by 1350. Interestingly, at least one later family member, Alexander Ramsay, was also a physician to royalty – James VI and Charles I.

There are a couple of sites on the estate where there may have been an early settlement: a wooden bailey on top of a natural mound or motte in one case and a late Iron Age/early medieval homestead on the other, the latter pre-dating the arrival of the Ramsays. The first references to a tower house at Bamff are made in charters dated 1580 and 1595 and Pont's map of Perthshire shows an L-shaped tower there at that time. During the 18th century considerable changes were made: a sketch of 1828, when the east range of the house was added, shows a double flight of steps leading to the front door on the first floor. Various details were added to give the house a classical look from the outside, the tower was restructured considerably within and the fenestration changed. After 1828 the next significant changes to the house took place in 1842, when William Burn and David Bryce remodelled it. The space in front of the house was blasted out and the front door placed in a new hall, which had been extended beyond the old front wall of the building. The east side of the house was extended northward with the addition of a new dining room and butler's pantry. The upper windows were given half dormers and crow-steps were added to all the gables, giving the house a more baronial look, as was very much the fashion at the time. In 1926 Sir Douglas Ramsay added a floor to the east side of the house, and there the development of Bamff House stood until the present generation inherited the estate in 1986 and further modernisation and extension took place.

The present owners have also been active in the management of the wildlife on the 1300-acre estate, re-introducing beaver and wild boar. Apartments at Bamff are available for self-catering holidays.

The original tower is late 16th century but there are substantial later additions.

Grampians

The capital of the Grampian Highlands in Scotland's north-east is Aberdeen, the third-largest city after Glasgow and Edinburgh. Known these days as Scotland's "castle and whisky country" the region incorporates Banff and Buchan, Gordon, Kincardine and Deeside and Moray, in addition to Aberdeen, and takes its name from the Grampian mountain range. Covering almost half of the land area of Scotland the Grampians extend from the Highland Boundary Fault to Glen Mor (the Great Glen), and incorporate the Cairngorms and the Lochaber hills. The range includes Ben Nevis, at 1,344 metres the highest mountain in Britain, and Ben Macdui, the second highest at 1,309 metres. The Great Glen provides a natural boundary between the Highlands and the central and Grampian regions and contributes to the strategic significance of this northerly part of the region.

There has been human settlement around the mouths of the Dee and the Don for over 8,000 years but the "modern" Aberdeen was born in 1319 when it was granted royal *burgh* status by Robert the Bruce following his eviction of the occupying English from the city during the Wars of Scottish Independence, in 1308. At this time it seems he also burned down and eradicated all trace of Aberdeen's castle. The area was at the centre of much fighting over succeeding centuries, including incursions by the English (though not to the extent suffered in the Borders), attacks by local warlords, and the fights between Royalists and the Covenantors. Aberdeen's city gates were not removed until 1770.

In the immediate vicinity of Aberdeen is a group of 13 castles of various ages, promoted to today's tourists as *the castle trail*. This concentration of fortified buildings is evidence of the importance of the area over a considerable period of time. They include Fyvie, Corgarff, Huntly, Crathes, Drum and Delgatie.

The 15th century castle of Balmoral was bought by Queen Victoria in 1852 for a little over £30,000. It is situated in this region in the area now known as Royal Deeside, and the estate extends to over 50,000 acres. The queen's enthusiasm for Scotland was infectious and the example set by her in rebuilding Balmoral led to the remodelling in the romantic baronial style of many more of Scotland's ancient castles. She and Prince Albert had the original mansion, dating back to the 1480s, totally demolished and had a new "fairy-tale" neo-gothic castle built, complete with towers, turrets and crenellations. Much of what we now perceive to be typically Scottish actually dates from the Victorian period.

David I (1124-53) granted *burgh* status to Perth, in the south of this region, in the early 12th century, though the town and its immediate surrounds had been settled long before that time. Perth was then one of the wealthiest trading centres in Scotland. It boasted a royal castle but this was destroyed in a flood in the year 1209. It remained, however, a sufficiently important town to be fought over by the Scots and the English many times over the next few centuries.

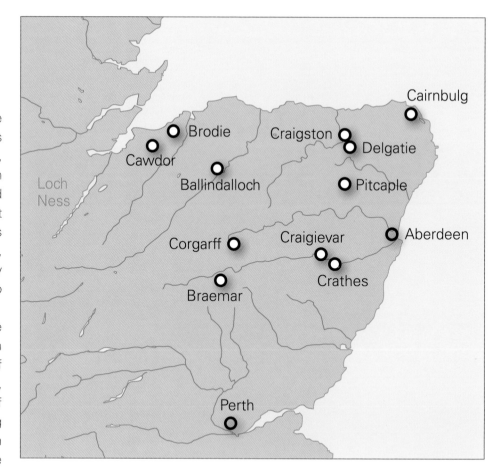

To the north of the region on the banks of the Moray Firth at the mouth of the river Ness, is the city of Inverness. The name is Gaelic and the area has been settled at least since the 6th century, when it was a Pictish stronghold, earning its royal charter some 700 years later. Legend has it that Macbeth murdered Duncan at Inverness castle, a building which was razed then rebuilt by Malcolm III. No trace remains of these structures. In the mid-16th century the then Earl of Huntly built a castle here. One of his relatives, a governor of the castle, refused admission to Mary Queen of Scots in 1562 and was subsequently executed for his treason. Through the civil war the castle generally held out against the Royalists and throughout the Jacobite risings remained under British control. Just outside the city lies Culloden moor, site of the battle of Culloden which finally ended the Jacobite uprisings in 1746. This was, coincidentally, also the last battle ever fought in mainland Britain. The present castle, on a cliff overlooking the river, is another example of the work of the ubiquitous Scottish architect, William Burn. A fine and grand demonstration of the Scottish baronial, in red sandstone, it was completed in 1836.

Loch Ness is of course also close by. At over 700 feet deep it contains more fresh water than all the lakes of England and Wales combined, so has plenty of room for the monster to hide. Urquhart Castle, once one of the largest in medieval Scotland, but now a ruin, stands on its westerly shore.

Craigievar

Craigievar, five miles south of Alford in Aberdeenshire, is a most unusual castle: built by William Forbes, a businessman rather than a nobleman, in the early 1600s, it has remained almost unchanged. Forbes was the brother of the Bishop of Aberdeen and was a highly successful import-export merchant. The de Forbes family became landed gentry with a grant of estates in Aberdeenshire from Alexander III in 1272. The owner of Craigievar was the younger son of William Forbes, 4th Laird of Corse, and was known as "Merchant WIllie" of Danzig, or "Danzig Willie". He purchased Craigievar Castle in around 1606 while it was still under construction by the Mortimers, a Norman-French family who had owned the estate for centuries but who had run into financial difficulties.

The castle was completed by 1626 and descendants of Forbes lived there until 1963 when it was bought by the National Trust for Scotland, for £30,000. It was built at a moment in history when Scotland was entering an unusual period of peace and prosperity. The rule of James VI in Scotland saw a marked reduction in feuding, and his accession as James I of England led to improved relations between the two countries. Nonetheless Craigievar, although comfortable by the standards of the time, was still designed with an awareness that trouble could be lurking just around the corner. This does however apply more to the lower storeys than the upper, where the castle begins to display more concern with luxury than with defence. There are large light windows throughout and a conspicuous absence of gun-loops. The biggest difference between early and late period tower houses, however, is found right at the top. Here at Craigievar there are no wall-walks, battlements or machicolations of the late middle ages; instead we see towers and turrets which look now as charming and fanciful as they must have done to Forbes, almost 400 years ago. A coat of arms over the main staircase is dated from 1668 and shows the Forbes family motto: „Doe not vaiken sleiping dogs."

Originally the lower storeys of this six-floored granite building would have been without windows, to maintain defences. The top floors, however, are a delightful example of the Scottish Baronial style, with extensive turrets, cupolas and corbelling on one of the last tower-houses ever built. It was originally surrounded by a walled courtyard that had a round tower at each corner, only one of which still remains. The Laird of the castle and his family occupied the top part of the castle, while soldiers and staff lived in the lower part where the kitchen fires were kept burning, allowing heat to rise to the Laird's quarters. There is just one entrance and it is said that although the Forbes might enter through the main door, they all had finally to leave through a window as it was impossible to carry a coffin down the narrow stairs.

The castle managed to withstand many attacks and sieges over the centuries, a testimonty to its robust design. The great hall boasts a secret staircase, a musicians´ gallery and a large fireplace with the Stuart arms. Original painted ceilings have survived the passing of the centuries in remarkably good condition, as has a collection of family portraits and furniture dating back to the 17th century.

Ballindalloch

Ballindalloch castle built between the rivers Spey and Avon in Banffshire has been the home of various different lines of the Grant family (now the MacPherson-Grants) since at least 1561. The date carved on a fireplace within the building shows that it was already standing by 1546 though what appears to be the original entrance has a date of 1602. Ballindalloch is known as *the pearl of the north* and stands close by the whisky distilleries of Glenlivet and Glenfiddich. The original building was a Z-plan fortified tower, seriously damaged and plundered by the Marquess of Montrose in 1645, rebuilt and further extended and improved over the following three centuries. One of the most famous members of the family was General James Grant, who fought in the American Wars of Independence. In 1763, he was appointed Governor of Florida, a position he held until 1771. His grand-nephew, George Macpherson of Invereshie inherited the estates and in 1838 was created Sir George Macpherson-Grant, 1st Baronet of Ballindalloch. By taking both family names, Sir George symbolically united the two great clans of Strathspey. He and his son made major additions to the castle in the second half of the 19th century and it was on their farm that the world-renowned Aberdeen Angus cattle was first bred. The name Macpherson has an unusual derivation. In the 12th century one Ewan Ban was Abbot of Kingussie. His elder brother died and he became head of Clan Chattan but could not combine this with his religious duties. The Pope granted him dispensation to marry, and his son became known as Macpherson, son of the parson.

The initials of Grant and MacPherson.

The dovecote (or *doocot*): pigeons were an important source of food.

The Grants' and Macphersons' coats of arms are combined here above the doorway.

Ballindalloch was substantially rebuilt after a fire in 1645. The original Z-plan castle had been built a hundred years earlier.

An ornate but comfortable study, decorated in 19th century style, with a fine collection of stuffed birds of prey.

Ballindalloch has all the "Scottish" architectural features.

A detail of the elegant and well-preserved corbelling.

General James Grant fought in the American Wars of Independence.

The Braemar region is mountainous: it sits in the midst of the Cairngorms and boasts over 24 Munros (mountains over 3000 feet), the whole area lying at least 1000 feet above sea level.

Braemar

Home today to the head of the Farquharson clan, Braemar was originally built by John Erskine, 2nd Earl of Mar in 1628. In medieval times Braemar was at the crossroads of two important routes between Aberdeenshire and Perthshire and the route from the north to Angus. Other routes of lesser importance also converged on Braemar, so that whoever controlled that area was in a position of great strength. Mar built the castle both as a hunting lodge and to defend his estates against his neighbours, the Farquharsons. They fought each other during the Glorious Revolution in 1688-9, Farquharson's Jacobite troops initially taking the castle. It was then re-captured by the Government troops who were soon driven out again, and at this point Farquharson set fire to Braemar, to prevent its being used by the enemy in the future. It remained a ruin for 60 years until it was bought by John Farquharson, 9th Laird of Invercauld, in 1732. Despite coming out rather half-heartedly on the Jacobite side in 1715, the Farquharsons just avoided being on the losing side at Culloden and were fairly well-treated, being allowed to retain ownership of Braemar after agreeing to its rebuilding and use as a Hanoverian garrison. In 1748 reconstruction was put in hand and the castle gained its star-shaped defensive walls. Troops finally moved out in 1797. The Braemar region is mountainous: it sits in the midst of the Cairngorms and boasts over 24 Munros (mountains over 3000 feet), the whole area lying at least 1000 feet above sea level.

A soldier billeted here in the 1750s carved his name on the shutters.

The castle was built in the 1600s and has changed little over the years.

The dungeon – a tiny hole beneath the floor, used as recently as 1820.

The star-shaped defensive walls were added in 1748 when Braemar became a barracks for Hanoverian troops. It continued to be used by troops for almost 50 years.

In 1875 the 12th Laird Farquarson moved back into Braemar and it reverted from its use as a barracks for almost a hundred years, to family home.

Brodie

Brodie Castle is located 4½ miles west of Forres and 24 miles east of Inverness on the east coast of Scotland. Built in 1567, it was badly damaged by fire in 1645, and substantially rebuilt, the lime-harled building being a typical Z-plan tower house with ornate corbelled battlements, crow-step gables and conical-roofed towers. An eastern wing was added to the house in the 19th century. The Brodies held their lands here for over 800 years and may even be descendants of the Pictish royal house of Brude. Malcolm IV granted various lands to the Thanes of Brodie in 1160 and their position was further strengthened by Robert the Bruce, who they supported at Bannockburn. Unfortunately all the family papers detailing their history were lost in the fire at the castle in 1645. It is known however that they were staunch Protestants, Covenantors – which led to the burning of the castle in 1645 – and that they picked the winning side in 1745. The castle now belongs to The National Trust for Scotland and has an extensive collection of art and furniture.

In the grounds of the castle stands *Rodney's Stone*, a six-foot high Pictish stone which was originally found in the nearby grounds of the old church of Dyke and Moy. It has a cross on one face, and symbols on the other – two fish monsters and, below, a "Pictish Beast" and other Pictish symbols. On the other face are a cross and some animals. Both faces carry a long inscription.

One of the two 5-storey towers at the corners of the 17th century keep. The castle was substantially extended in 1824, without loss of the older features.

Brodie Castle was home to the Brodie family from the 1500s to the late 20th century. The family's association with the region goes back to the 1100s.

The massive square tower to the left of the photograph was built around 1380, with the round tower to the right being added in the mid-16th century.

Cairnbulg

Cairnbulg Castle is the family seat of the Frasers of Philorth, Lords Saltoun. It is probable that at the time it was built, it was on the estuary of the Water of Philorth, and its original name, Philorth, means "Pool of the river Orth". Until the early 14th century the Comyns, Earls of Buchan, owned all the land in this part of Aberdeenshire which is still known as Buchan. Before the battle of Largs in 1263 and the defeat of the Norsemen the coast of Buchan had been exposed to regular invasions. The Earls of Buchan were responsible for coastal defence and built various castles round the coast of which the first stone castle on the site of Philorth / Cairnbulg was probably one. Over the past few hundred years the sea along this part of the coast has been constantly receding, so that the castle no longer seems associated with coastal defences.

In the Wars of Independence, the Comyns fought with the English against Robert the Bruce, and after his victory in 1309, he carried out an operation known as the *harrying of Buchan*, destroying all the castles of the Earldom, so that they could never again be held against him. The Earl of Ross, one of Robert's supporters was given this part of Buchan and the ruins of the castle. Around 1380 the rectangular tower was built and was part of the dowry of the then Earl's daughter on her marriage to Sir Alexander Fraser.

The foundations for this massive tower were simply huge boulders laid upon the underlying clay. The round tower was added in the mid-16th century at the same time as similar additions were being made at Balvenie, Strathbogie, Newark and Kirkwall.

Sir Alexander Fraser built the town of Fraserburgh, improved the harbour, founded a university there and built another castle; as a result he got heavily into debt, leading to the selling of Cairnbulg to another branch of the family in 1613. Ownership passed out of the family and by the late 18th century the castle was a ruin. It was restored in the late 1800s and repurchased by the Saltouns in the 1930s. Cairnbulg is one of the oldest castles still lived in by the family who built it, the Frasers.

Next page: After 1775 this splendid castle was vandalised, left empty and became a ruin, until its renovation in 1896 by Sir John Duthie. Ownership reverted to the Frasers – Lord Saltoun – in 1934.

The interior has been substantially refurbished since the 1960s.

The portrait collection includes every laird since 1570.

The castle slowly fell into ruin after the early 1700s, as this painting shows. It was substantially rebuilt in the late 1800s by its then owner, Sir John Duthie.

Cawdor

The main tower, built in 1460, is part of a complex begun one hundred years earlier by the Thanes of Cawdor and extended during the reign of James III. The tower was originally surrounded by a ditch, superseded by a moat and drawbridge. An earlier fortification on a nearby site, built by William the Lion in 1179, was intended to control the ford over the river Nairn and protect the coastal route between Inverness and Elgin. The titles Thane and Earl are two of the oldest baronial ranks, deriving from the Norse words *thegn* and *jarl*. Thane equates to the English *baron* and indicated a trusted, land-owning servant of the king with responsibility for local administration and law-enforcement, and the maintenance of a fighting force – and answerable only to the king. The Thanes of Calder (Cawdor) were appointed sheriffs and hereditary constables of the castle at Nairn. The tall, stone-built successor building with its plain rectangular tower-house with only one entrance to the outside world set at upper first floor level was clearly intended to keep out unwelcome guests.

This Castle hath a pleasant seat; the air
Nimbly and sweetly recommends itself
Unto our gentle senses

William Shakespeare, *Macbeth*

The original entrance to Cawdor was via a first floor door, the outline of which can be seen here above the later wall.

This window is in the complex of buildings surrounding the tower, which contains the kitchens and dining area, and various drawing and dressing rooms.

90

The Thane decided to build a new castle. Following a dream, he loaded a coffer of gold on to the back of a donkey and let it roam: where the animal lay down to rest in the evening he would build. The donkey lay down under the thorn tree which can still be seen inside Cawdor today.

Corgarff sits on a low hill surrounded by open space. This gave good protection against artillery attack but did not prevent the castle´s being burned on at least three occasions.

Corgarff

Corgarff is spectacular for its setting, in the middle of the vast open space high in Strathdon on the northern edge of the Cairngorms. It did however dominate an important road much used by drovers and raiders and has had a turbulent history. It is a plain rectangular towerhouse and was built by the Forbes clan in around 1550.

From 1607 the castle became the headquarters of local bandits who plundered the surrounding area until 1626 when it was acquired by the Earl of Mar, of one of Scotland's most ancient noble families. In 1645 it was used as the mustering point by the Marquis of Montrose, commander of the Royalist forces in Scotland during the Civil War. During the 1689 rising Corgarff was again burned down, this time by Jacobites to prevent its being used as a base by supporters of William of Orange. The Earl of Mar used Corgarff as a headquarters for his troops during the 1715 rising and, having lost, found the castle once more burned down and the Mar estates forfeited. The government returned it to the Forbes family but again in 1745 they found themselves on the wrong side and the castle reverted to government hands, becoming a barracks in 1748, two years after Culloden. At this juncture the star-shaped outer defensive wall was added, complete with gun loops. The castle was however never attacked again. Corgarff's last governmental function was as a base for officers attempting to suppress illegal whisky distilling in the early 1800s. The army left in 1831 and the last inhabitants abandoned the castle during the first world war. It is now maintained by Historic Scotland.

There is nowhere in the star-shaped outer wall which does not afford defenders at least two angles of fire.

Corgarff was last inhabited in the 1890s. It was restored in the 1960s and is now maintained by Historic Scotland.

The red stone quoins at Craigston were clearly intended as a feature and the use of whitewash achieves the objective, making a very unusual and distinctive building.

Craigston

Despite being unambiguously a tower house, Craigston, built four miles north-east of Turriff, in Aberdeenshire, in 1617, was designed for comfort and for show rather than as a fortalice. Built by, and still owned by the Urquhart family, whose Barony at the time was of *Craigfintray*, this was a C-plan rather than the more common Z-plan structure. The whole thing was constructed in under four years – decidedly speedy for the time – by John Urquhart of Craigfintray, known as the Tutor of Cromarty. Until he was granted the barony and estates of Craigfintray in 1597 the Urquhart family's principal landholdings were at Cromarty, then an important fishing and trading port on the Black Isle. The Tutor's direct descendants were at worst profligate, at best not very good with money, and by 1657 the castle had to be sold, returning to Urquhart ownership in the early 18th century.

Craigston has some unusual design features. The massive red stone quoins were clearly designed to be left exposed and on the present whitewashed structure represent a very distinctive feature. There is corbelling on the four outer angles where one would expect protective towers: there is however no sign of there ever having been any. The arch between the two wings encloses a long gallery and the entrance arch below is a much later addition. The two exterior wings were added in the mid-1700s by captain John Urquhart (aka *the pirate*) who seems to have made most of his fortune from privateering (a euphemism for legalized piracy). An attractive but, in historical terms, less significant castle than many.

The drawing room windows afford views over the extensive parklands.

The wings were added in the 1700s by John "the pirate" Urquhart.

A bowl featuring Bonnie Prince Charlie, given to the family after 1745.

The wooden panel with a carving of Robert the Bruce was
moved to the new drawing room in the 1750s.

The plaque over the window records the fact that this castle was built
over the unusually short period of under four years.

An engraving of Sir Thomas Urquhart, a soldier and a scholar,
known as The Great Sir Thomas. He died in 1660.

One of the many bedrooms at Craigston.

The pirate collected art and subsequent generations have enhanced the collection.

The distinctive carving stands out against the whitewashed wall.

The library is built into the gallery, way above the front door.

Crathes

Crathes, like Craigievar and Craigston was a tower house, built by the Burnetts to demonstrate wealth and success, rather than for its defensive qualities. Like Craigievar, the lower storeys have a defensive appearance, while the upper storeys have a variety of corbelling and turrets. Crathes was begun in 1553 and, in stark contrast to Craigston took 43 years to complete. The castle, an L-plan tower house, boasts painted ceilings dating from the second half of the 17th century and a fine 18th century garden. The walled gardens are almost as famous as the castle itself and extend to the south-east of the castle forming an oblong covering 3.75 acres, twice as long from north to south as from east to west.

The Burnetts seem to have been a canny family, retaining good relationships with both sides in most conflicts, so that the castle was never destroyed by hostile forces. Indeed, during the civil war Sir Thomas Burnett managed to obtain letters from both royalists and parliamentarians confirming that Crathes and the Burnetts should not be molested: these documents remain on view at Crathes today.

The 3rd Baronet, Thomas Burnett, married Margaret Arbuthnott in the 1680s, and in just 22 years they had 21 children. Sir Thomas and Lady Margaret thoughtfully added a three-storey wing to the east of the castle to house their progeny. This burned down in 1966, and was replaced by the two-storey wing which stands there today. Sir James Burnett of Leys donated the castle, gardens and surrounding woodlands and fields to The National Trust for Scotland in 1951.

The decorative sash windows are a later addition to the 17th century tower.

Crathes was designed as an impressive family home, rather than as a fortified castle.

Crathes, now owned by the National Trust for Scotland, is one of the country's best-preserved castles. The two-storey wing was added in the 18th century.

The huge five-foot wide staircase was part of the original 1540s structure and is built within the width of the wall of the castle.

Delgatie

By the mid-20th century Delgatie, which has a claim to being the oldest inhabited house in Britain, was almost a ruin. It was first built by the Comyns, the Earls of Buchan, in about 1030, passing to the Hay family after Bannockburn, in 1314. Sir Gilbert Hay, the 5th Lord Erroll, fought for Robert the Bruce and as his reward he was made the Lord High Constable of Scotland, a title formerly held by the Comyns and which the Clan Hay continues to hold to this day: the title gives them ceremonial precedence in Scotland ahead of anyone but the royal family.

The Hay family can trace its roots to the Normandy village of La Haye-Bellefond. Haye means a hedge, and thus the defensive wooden stockade which often surrounded Norman castles. William de la Haye, Butler of Scotland and first baron of Erroll, arrived in Scotland around 1160. He married the Celtic heiress Eva whose dowry was the Erroll lands while his son married Ethna, daughter of the Earl of Strathearn.

The main structure of the present castle dates from this time, though it was significantly strengthened in the 1500s. The Hays were Catholic and sided with the Covenantors, and the castle was at the heart of several attacks and sieges: after one the west wall had to be rebuilt but under James VI's laws it could be no thicker than an arrow's length: previously it had been over ten feet thick (three metres). Two wings were added in the 18th century.

This magnificent painted ceiling was finished in 1597.

Like many old Scottish houses, Delgatie has its dovecote – or *doocot*.

The ballroom was rebuilt by the 8th Earl at the end of the 16th century.

The grounds of this ancient house are littered with statuary, guns and structures in varying stages of disrepair.
The cannon was used in the Indian Mutiny of 1857. The stone cannonballs were used in a siege of Dalgetie in 1594.

The Hay family were granted the castle when it was forfeited to Robert the Bruce, after Bannockburn, by the Earls of Buchan, the Comyns. The basic structure is thought to date from the 14th century.

Pitcaple

Pitcaple castle, on the river Urie, in central Aberdeenshire, is built on land given by James II in 1457 to David Leslie, the first Baron of Pitcaple and eldest son of Sir William Leslie, 4th Baron of Balquhain. Pitcaple stands just two miles from the Castle of Balquhain and it remained in the family until 1757 when the last of the Leslies, Brigadier General Sir James Leslie died. The castle then passed to James's daughter who was married to Professor John Lumsden. It remained in the Lumsden family until the latter part of the 20th century when Margaret, on her marriage to Captain Patrick Burges, obtained permission to change the family name to Burges-Lumsden.

This splendid house has all the "Scottish" features: towers with conical (actually concave – see below) roofs, crow-stepped gables, corner turrets with corbelling – and harling. It was built in the second half of the 15th century and originally comprised the circular Thane's Tower. This was extended into the familiar Z-plan shape in the 1640s, after a turbulent period involving skirmishes with Covenantors. To provide further protection the height of the towers was raised and a moat was added – though this feature no longer exists. Hugh Lumsden transformed the castle into a Scottish vernacular country house in the 1830s: the concave roofs were added to the towers at this time and are clearly French-influenced. His son built a further wing in 1872 to house his 12 children.

In 1457, by this charter, James II confirmed ownership of Pitcaple by the Leslies of Balquhain.

The Lumsden family motto translates as "Thank God I am what I am."

The entrance hall, in the new wing, was remodelled in 1872.

Sir William Burn was hired to renovate the castle in the 1870s. Pitcaple is now considered to be one of the finest examples of the Scottish vernacular style.

Clothes worn by various members of the Lumsden Family, displayed in a little museum on the top floor of the castle.

A cross between a black grouse and a capercaillie, shot on Benachie by Rear Admiral Walter Lumsden in 1900.

Highlands and the West

The Great Glen divides the Grampian Mountains to the south-east from the Highlands to the north-west. This was always a remote region, unconquered by the Romans and long out of reach of the English. The Scottish Reformation began in the Lowlands but only partial success was achieved in the Gaelic-speaking Highlands where Roman Catholicism and antipathy towards the Protestant English remained strong. Most Lowland Scots converted to Protestantism and were more willing to unite with the English to create the United Kingdom. Culturally the region remained apart from the rest of Scotland until the last hundred years or so.

Culloden Moor is in the Highlands, near Inverness and many (but by no means all) of the Highland clans turned out in force in 1746 to fight the English. Over the period preceding and following Culloden the spirit of the highlanders was severely weakened by the appalling behaviour of the Duke of Cumberland's armies. He is said to have instructed his troops to "show no quarter" in battle but this level of inhumanity extended also to their behaviour towards civilians. Men, women and children were killed, made homeless and robbed of their cattle, horses and few possessions in the quest to "control the rebels". The Highlands are remembered also for the clearances of the 18th and early 19th centuries when the British (and some of the Scottish) establishment used the screen of agricultural efficiency to attempt to destroy, once and for all, the archaic, militaristic clan system, which they believed had facilitated the Jacobite Risings. In the space of around 50 years, the Highlands became one of the most sparsely populated areas in Europe. Ordinary homes and farmsteads were also destroyed so that few buildings older than 19th century – other than castles – remain standing today.

In the western part of the region the old enemy was not England but Norway. The Vikings had raided England and the East coast since the 8th century but found their way into the western Isles in the early 800s. Settlers from Norway sailed to the Shetlands, the Orkneys, the Hebridies, the Isle of Man, the Western Islands, and parts of the Scottish mainland. The land and climate were similar to that at home and it was close to existing Viking settlements in Ireland and England. The Vikings intermarried with the native Celtic and Pictish populations and had a lasting influence on the language and culture of the region. The Vikings established territories known as *jarldoms* (English 'earldoms') under the ultimate sovereignty of the kings of Norway. This continued unchanged until the Viking defeat at the Battle of Largs in 1263, when Norway surrendered control of the islands, Kintyre and Man, to the Scottish crown. Norse control lasted longest in Shetland, which was ruled directly from Norway until the 15th century. The activity hereabouts led to the construction of the earliest surviving stone castles, such as Sween and Tioram, crude structures with massive walls and few windows, situated where the enemy could be seen from a distance, with sheer size being the sole defence.

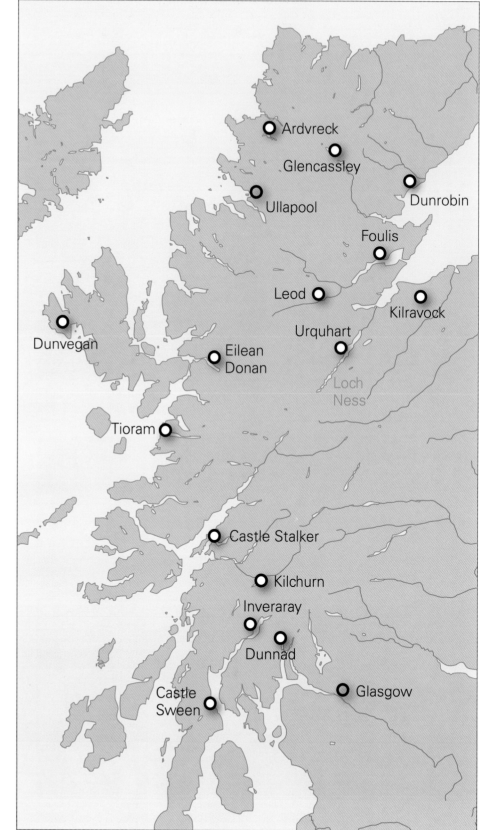

Inveraray

Inveraray Castle is home to the Campbells, subsequently Earls and Dukes of Argyll, who first settled in Argyllshire in 1220. They moved from Innischonnell on Loch Awe to Inveraray in the 1400s. It was the Earl's regiment which carried out the notorious massacre of Glencoe, which earned him his Dukedom in 1701. The building of the present massive baroque castle began in 1720 based on a sketch by Vanburgh, architect of Blenheim Palace and Castle Howard. It was completed in 1789.

Ardvreck

The ruins of Ardvreck Castle stand at the east end of Loch Assynt, close by the shell of Calda House. Ardvreck was built in 1490 by the MacLeods of Assynt and replaced in 1726 by Calda House, built using some of the stone from Ardvreck. It was originally a three-storey tower house with a corbelled section housing the main staircase and a vaulted basement. Across the narrow neck of the promontory is a dry stone wall that marks the line of an old defensive wall which will itself have been further protected by a ditch.

Inveraray Castle incorporates Baroque, Palladian and Gothic styles.

Just enough remains of Ardvreck to identify it as having once been a three-storey tower house.

Dunrobin

Dunrobin Castle, with 189 rooms, is the largest house in the northern Highlands. It is situated a mile north of Golspie in Sutherland on the east coast of northern Scotland, about 90 minutes north of Inverness. Despite its relatively modern appearance, parts of this beautiful, French-style castle overlooking the North Sea date back to the 1300s. It is the seat of the Earls of Sutherland, the longest-established Earls in Scotland. They were granted their lands by David I in the early 1100s and were created Earls around a hundred years later. The central tower of today's castle was built some 40 years later (though substantially rebuilt in 1401). The three main sections of Dunrobin were built in the late 16th century, the late 18th century and finally in the mid-1800s when Sir Charles Barry (architect of the Houses of Parliament, in London) remodelled the whole of the castle in the distinctly French-Scottish style with tall, conical roofs, creating a substantial additional section and laying out the formal gardens. The location, on a hilltop overlooking the sea, indicates its original defensive function, as does the massive sloping stone plinth (the *batter*) on which the building stands.

It is said that the daughter of the 14th Earl of Sutherland fell in love with a man that her father considered unsuitable. The Earl locked his daughter in an attic room to prevent her from eloping. She tried to escape by climbing down a rope but her father surprised her and she fell to her death and now she haunts the upper floors of the castle.

The tower seen through this window is the oldest surviving part of the castle.

This section of the castle is part of the Victorian additions, by Sir Charles Barry, built between 1845 and 1850.

The castle stands on a hill with open views across the sea, in an ideal defensive position.

The white section of Dunrobin was completed in the late 1600s, the middle section 100 years later and the part to the right in 1850.
The whole is very influenced by French architectural style.

Standing on one of the oldest sites of any Scottish castle, Dunrobin once included huge estates, most of which had to be sold in 1921 to pay off family debts.

The library was remodelled by Scottish architect Sir Robert Lorrimer following a fire in 1915. During this early part of the first world war the room was in use as a hospital.

The castle's rebuilding in the 19ᵗʰ century was much influenced by Balmoral and the popular Scottish baronial style.

The title of Earl of Sutherland goes back to around 1230. This and other family titles are recorded on coats of arms around the castle.

Dunvegan

Dunvegan Castle has been the home of clan MacLeod for over 800 years. In the 13th century Leod, son of Olaf the Black, built the MacLeod's first fortification - a curtain wall – on this loch-side site on the Isle of Skye, but there may well have been an older structure here as the old Norse *dun-* generally indicated a fortified hill. Building work has been carried out in almost every century since, the predominant features of the current castle being a 14th century square keep, and a 16th century tower -- the Fairy Tower -- and another half-block from the 17th century. In common with many other castles, Dunvegan was extensively remodelled in the 19th century having crenellations and ornamental bartizans (small, overhanging turrets on a wall or tower) added back, in fanciful form, as decorations, rather than as genuine defensive features. The castle sits on a rocky outcrop which was, until the 18th century, separated from the mainland by a moat with the only access to the castle being from Loch Dunvegan. In the castle visitors can see the tattered remains of the Fairy Flag: it was said that this sacred banner, believed to date from the 7th century, would guarantee victory to the clan if unfurled in an emergency. However, the charm will only work on three occasions and it has already been used twice to secure MacLeod victories in battle. It is also said that every ten years at midnight on midsummer's day, the king of the fairies and all his court come to see the flag, and that any mortal who spies on them during this visit will die.

A view across the loch from the first barracks of The Black Watch.

The 16th century Dunvegan Cup, given to the MacLeods by grateful Ulstermen.

A dining table befitting one of the largest clans in the Highlands, the MacLeods. The walls are hung with just some of the castle's collection of family portraits.

Although this is without doubt a defensive structure, the bartizans and crenellations are a fanciful Victorian addition.

Eilean Donan

Eilean Donan in Loch Duich, on the west coast of Scotland and not far from the Isle of Skye, may well sit upon a very early fortified site. Opposite the castle is the sculptured impression of a human foot in a stone. Carvings like this have been found in other parts of Scotland at the entrance to Iron Age settlements. The name of the castle, and the island upon which it is built, derive from a 7th century Irish missionary, Donan, killed on Eigg in 618 AD; *eilean* is Gaelic for *island*. There have been several churches dedicated to Donan in the area. There had been Celtic missionary saints in the Western Isles and on the coast from the 5th century onwards but it seems that there were scarcely any cases of violent opposition, until the Viking and Danish raids began at the end of the 9th century. The pagan Celts accepted the missionaries even when they did not adopt their religion and pagan and Christian symbols are found side by side on the great Pictish stones.

The earliest records of a castle here are from the mid-1200s, just before the Norsemen finally withdrew from western Scotland. Since the 9th century and until around 1500, this region was part of the quite separate kingdom under the King – later the Lord – of the Isles and Eilean Donan witnessed prolonged feuding between the Mackenzie, Macrae and Macdonald clans; yet around the end of the 14th century the area of the castle was reduced to about a fifth of its original size. In 1719 it was bombarded by three English frigates as a force of Spanish soldiers, Stuart supporters, were garrisoned there: the warships caused a huge amount of damage but did not destroy it. The crews of the ships went ashore and fought their way into the keep, using the hundreds of barrels of gunpowder they discovered there to blow the building up. The ruins were not restored until the early 20th century, the rebuilding being completed in 1932. It is now one of the most photographed castles in the Highlands.

Despite being now essentially a 20th century structure, Eilean Donan is one of the most picturesque castles in Scotland.

Foulis Castle had to be rebuilt in 1745 following its destruction by Jacobite forces.

Foulis

Foulis (pronounced *fowls*) Castle has been the seat of the Munro clan for over 800 years. The castle, near Evanton in Ross-shire, was originally granted to them for services rendered in the defeat of Viking raiders and there are remains of an 11th century motte structure in the present castle grounds. The land hereabouts was called Estirfowlys (whence Foulis) with the Tower of Strathskehech built upon it. The fortalice survived as the home of the Munros until the 1745 rising when the Jacobite forces attacked and burned the castle. The then owner Sir Harry Munro built the present Georgian house on the ruins of the castle and the heraldic panel above the entrance bears the date 1777.

The 18th century façade gives no hint of Foulis' violent history.

Highland cattle enjoying some winter sunshine.

A 16th century gun loop in the five-foot thick tower wall.

The castle still houses many domestic and everyday artifacts, as well as grander works of art.

Sir Harry Munro of Foulis, 7th Baronet, 1725-1781.

Pots and kettles on the old wood-burning range.

The old kitchens at Foulis were still the family's only cooking facility as recently as 1948.

This stag was shot by David Lloyd, well-known rifle-maker, whose family owned Glencassley until 1998.

The gun-room, with its typical clutter of guns, saddles and waterproof clothing and hunting trophies.

Glencassley

Prior to 1870 Glencassley was part of the Rosehall estate in Sutherland. In a remote part of the Highlands, Rosehall was, interestingly, one of a group of local estates to try sheep-farming, commonly assumed to have been introduced only after the clearances of the early 19th century. Yet in 1788 the estate was let on a 38-year lease – at over £100 per annum – for sheep-farming. It is not clear quite how successful this was as in a local court case of 1797 it is stated "everything on the farm seems to be going to confusion and the corns, sheep and cattle are liable to be carried off by any person who pleases to do so".

In 1870 the estate was bought and broken up by speculators wanting to cash in on the new demand for Scottish sporting (ie – stalking, shooting and fishing) estates which resulted from Queen Victoria's purchasing Balmoral. The game book of 1931 shows one summer shooting party bagging 515 grouse and 138 rabbits! The river Cassley ran through the original Rosehall estate but when it was broken up the developers ensured that the two banks of the river went to different buyers so that two sets of fishing rights could be established.

The nine-bedroomed castle dates from the 1870s and was built by the English brewer Charles Flower, founder of The Royal Shakespeare Company. The drawing room is still decorated with scenes from Macbeth, painted by scenery-painters from the theatre in Stratford-on-Avon. The establishment of a permanent theatre in Stratford for the performance of Shakespeare's plays had been discussed as early as 1769, when the first Shakespeare Festival was held to celebrate David Garrick's Jubilee, but it was not until 1875 that Charles Flower, whose brewery was in Stratford, launched a national fundraising campaign to build a theatre and personally donated the two-acre site on the banks of the Avon, where the famous theatre now stands. Flower died in 1892 but his nephew Sir Archibald Flower bought the estate back in 1936. Interestingly, he paid £16,000 whereas his uncle had paid £24,000 in 1870.

The family finally sold again in 1998 for a rather higher price. The sale took place two years after the death of the renowned riflemaker David Lloyd who spent most of his life at Glencassley. A keen deer-stalker, it is said that he shot more than 5,000 red deer stags, the vast majority of them with rifles he had built himself. This was however no gentleman amateur gunsmith, but the creator of a world-renowned range of high-quality, magazine-fed sporting rifles with integral scope sights and dependably high accuracy at long ranges. The Lloyd rifle was recently voted by *Shooting Times* as number 8 in its list of the top 12 Rifles of All Time (the Kalashnikov AK-47 was number 7).

The Royal Shakespeare Company connection was also maintained as Lloyd's wife, Evadne, became the longest-ever serving governor of the company. Their son Sampson Lloyd is a well-known photographer, now living in London…

The nine-bedroomed castle dates from the 1870s and was built by the English brewer Charles Flower, founder of The Royal Shakespeare Company.

Kilchurn was badly damaged by lightning in 1769 and left to fall to picturesque ruin.

Kilchurn

Sir Colin Campbell, the founder of the Glenorchy or Breadalbane branch of Clan Campbell 'was a man of high renown for military prowess and for the virtues of social and domestic life. He was a stream of many tides against the foes of the people, but like the gale that moves the heath to those who sought his aid.' Born about A.D. 1400 Colin Campbell was a soldier and a traveller, visiting Rome and even Cairo and the Holy Land. After the murder of James I in 1437 he was responsible for tracking down and bringing the assassins to justice and as a reward James II conferred upon him the barony of Lawers. In 1440 Sir Colin erected the Castle of Kilchurn (originally *Coalchuirn*) on a rocky promontory at the east end of Loch Awe, under the shadow of Ben Cruachan mountain. In fact, legend has it that the castle was erected under the supervision of Lady Campbell during her husband's seven-year absence on a crusade.

Over the following decades the Campbells became the most powerful clan in western Scotland, partly because of Sir Colin's ability to make a good marriage – he managed four of them! Hs eldest son, Duncan, known as *Donacha dhu na Curich*, Black Duncan o' the Cowl, proved equally adept at acquiring estates and staying close to the king (Charles I appointed Sir Duncan Baronet of Nova Scotia in 1625), and the Campbells continued to acquire wealth and influence. However Duncan's son Robert became a Covenantor and lost much of the estates in 1644-5. His grandson, John, became first Earl of Breadalbane and was described as a man "who could bring seventeen hundred claymores into the field...is as cunning as a fox, wise as a serpent, and slippery as an eel." It was he who, now a supporter of William & Mary, was paid to negotiate with the Jacobite supporters, a period culminating in the infamous Glencoe massacre of the Campbell's old enemies, the Macdonalds.

When first built Kilchurn was a five-storey castle with a curtain wall on an island, completely surrounded by water: land was reached through a subterranean passage – the loch's waters were lowered by a drainage scheme in 1817. Interestingly, household books from as early as 1590 survive and show what life was like for wealthy castle-dwellers of the time. This passage contains kitchen accounts of 1590: "the oatmeal consumed in the household was 364 bolls, the malt 207 bolls. They used 90 beeves, more than two-thirds consumed fresh; 20 swine, 200 sheep, 424 salmon from the native rivers; 15,000 herrings, 30 dozen of hard fish; 1,805 'heads' of cheese new and old, weighing 325 stone; and 9 stones of butter, 26 dozen loaves of wheaten bread... capons, geese, wild geese, brawn, venison, partridges, blackcock, 'birsell' fowls, and rabbits...claret wyne, quhyit (white) wine, Spanis wyne, ale..."

Because of its important strategic location the castle was altered in the 1690s to accommodate a barracks for the Earl's private army. It was occupied by Hanoverian troops during the Risings of 1715 and 1745 but, despite surviving the fighting, was badly damaged by lightning in 1769 and left to fall to picturesque ruin. Wordsworth called it: *this child of loud-throated war.*

The oldest part of Kilravock is the 15th century stone tower. The block beside it was added a hundred years later, though the windows are an 18th century addition.

Kilravock

The oldest part of Kilravock (pronounced *Kilrork*) castle is the square stone tower, built in 1460, some 150 years after the Norman Rose family settled in the area. The licence to build was granted by John, Lord of the Isles and Earl of Ross. *Kil* derives from the Celtic word for *church* and it is thought that St. Columba preached at an old chapel on this site, in 565 AD; there were several Christian churches built in the surrounding area at this time, marked today by place-names beginning with *Kil*. Despite having walls eight feet thick the tower was damaged and burned as early as 1482, by the rival Mackintoshes. In 1553 the 10th Laird added a substantial further wing, in part to help house his 17 sisters and daughters! The Queen Anne-style windows were put in in the early 18th century. The Rose family still lives at Kilravock today.

The *doocot* by the lake is said to be on the site where
St. Columba preached in 565 AD.

An 18th century painting showing how little has changed since then.

The door at the back of the great hall leads to the dungeons.

Leod

Castle Leod, an L-plan sandstone tower-house is the result of the re-building and re-design in 1606 of an older castle on the site. The name Leod would suggest that it belonged to the MacLeod clan but this is, in fact, the seat of the Mackenzies. Sir Roderick (Rory) Mackenzie had married Margaret MacLeod in 1605 and when he built this castle he incorporated the MacLeod coat of arms into that of his own family and gave the castle its name. Rory's grandson became the first Earl of Cromartie. The family were Jacobites and lost their title and estates – and, almost, their lives – after 1745. John Mackenzie however raised two battalions to support George III and was allowed to repurchase the estate for £19,000, in 1784, and Leod remains the headquarters of the Clan Mackenzie. Queen Victoria restored the titles to the family in 1849.

The Mackenzie – MacLeod marriage finally brought to an end a long-lasting violent feud between the two clans but the new castle was still intended as a most effective defensive structure, with walls seven to eight feet thick, iron grilles on the lower windows, and a host of arrow-slits, which must have been something of an anachronism by the early 17th century. There are also plenty of splayed gun loops and the entrance is guarded by shot-holes.

Arrow slit above, gun loop below and a bell to give warning.

The original sturdy oak door of the early 1600s has a massive lock on the inside and iron bands and studs on the outside.

The L-plan castle Leod was first built in 1605 by Sir Rory Mackenzie and his wife Margaret MacLeod.

Castle Stalker

The picturesque Castle Stalker, 25 miles north of Oban on the west coast of Scotland, has a fascinating and bloody history, at the very heart of a centuries-long feud between the Stewarts and the MacDonalds and various ongoing spats with the MacDougalls, Campbells and McLeans. The castle sits at the mouth of Loch Laich (by Loch Linnhe) on a rocky islet known as the Rock of the Cormorants, and was built around 1446 by Sir John Stewart, Lord of Lorn whose descendants became Chiefs of Appin. It could only ever be reached by boat. An earlier fortalice on the site had been built by the then Lord, a MacDougall, but the family lost their title and lands to the Stewarts in the late 14th century. In around 1620 the castle passed to the Campbells of Airds , one of whom won it in a drunken wager with the 7th Stewart Chief, Duncan, in exchange for a rowing boat! The Stewarts of Appin managed to regain the Castle in 1686, but only briefly: the Campbells got it back four years later and remained in residence until around 1800. They abandoned Stalker, the roof fell in and it became a ruin until renovated by the Stewart family in the 20th century. The name derives from the Celtic word for hunter.

The last Campbell was born in the Castle in 1775 but moved out of this inhospitable location 25 years later. In about 1840 the roof fell in and the Castle was finally abandoned. It was rebuilt in the late 20th century by descendants of Charles Stewart, who had purchased the ruin and thus returned it to family ownership, in 1908.

Tioram

Castle Tioram (pronounced *cheerum*), a fine and rare example of an early stone curtain-walled castle, is sited on the rocky tidal island of Eilean Tioram (the Dry Island) where the waters of Loch Moidart and the river Shiel meet. The curtain walls are probably from the 13th century, the tower and other buildings being a century or two younger. There are no arrow-slits in the castle's lower walls and the defence would have been primarily in the location of the place and the thickness of the walls. There is a small box machicolation over the entrance, from which an invader could be attacked from a great height, and all around the top of the walls there was a wooden platform, supported on projecting beams held in the holes still visible at the top of the walls.

Once a centre of power of the medieval Lordship of the Isles, and later of the Macdonalds of Clanranald, Tioram was burnt on the orders of the last chief of the clan when he set off to join the doomed Jacobite rising of 1715, in order to keep it out of the hands of the Hanoverian forces. It has never been lived in since then.

Castle Tioram is a fine and rare example of an early stone curtain-walled castle whose defence would have consisted primarily in the location of the place and the thickness of the walls.

Most of the present ruined buildings of Castle Urquhart date from around 1509 but there was
a very significant castle on this site for several hundred years before this time.

Urquhart

A big, sprawling complex on the banks of Loch Ness, Urquhart is unusually large for a Scottish castle. Archeological and documentary evidence show that this site was in continuous use from Pictish times (possibly even the Iron Age – at nearby Corrimony there is a burial cairn dating from about 2000 BC) until the castle's abandonment at the end of the 17th century. It almost certainly started life as a ring-work fort on a hilltop site, surrounded by rubble and wood walls. The first stone building here was erected in the early 13th century by Alan Durward, Earl of Atholl and a Norman knight and son-in-law of Alexander II. In 1275, after Durward had died without an heir under a grant from Edward I of England, it passed into the hands of the Comyn family who built on what is now known as the nether bailey. Twenty-one years thereafter Edward I had English troops garrisoned here and in 1297 Sir Andrew Moray tried to retake Urquhart from the English, and began what became known as the Wars of Independence. The Comyns and Urquhart played their part in this war with Robert the Bruce (crowned King of Scotland, in 1306) taking the castle from Alexander of Badenoch. The Comyns' enmity with Bruce lead to the loss of their lands and their influence in Scotland. Throughout the late 13th and early 14th centuries Castle Urquhart fell regularly to Clan MacDonald, the Lords of the Isles, only to be retaken again and again by the Crown.

Most of the present ruined buildings date from around 1509, when the castle passed into the hands of the Grants. The charter granted to Sir John Grant required him to build a castle with "a hall, a chamber and kitchen, with all the requisite offices, such as a pantry, bakehouse, brewhouse… and orchard, with the necessary wooden fences" which makes 16th century life sound quite bucolic, after the excitements of the preceding few hundred years. But at the time the whole castle, incorporating much of the original castle and the various defence-driven additions, will have constituted a very impressive structure indeed, though by the early 1600s it was in ruins and was substantially dismantled by locals for building materials.

There have, not surprisingly, been several sightings of the Loch Ness Monster from here! The castle is perfectly sited on a promontory on the north shore of the loch to give fine views in both directions. The loch itself, cutting a huge fissure known as *Glen Mor* – The Great Glen – across central Scotland, is over 700 feet deep and surrounded by steep slopes. Sightings of the monster date back to the report from the 7th century stating that St. Columba had rescued a local from the creature: "he raised his holy hand, while all the rest, brethren as well as strangers, were stupefied with terror, and, invoking the name of God, formed the saving sign of the cross in the air, and commanded the ferocious monster, saying, 'Thou shalt go no further, nor touch the man; go back with all speed.'

Perhaps not surprisingly, there have been several sightings of the Loch Ness monster from here.

Massive walls and small openings give protection from attack from the loch.

The South-West

This is the region south-west of Glasgow close to but not contiguous with the English border including Ayrshire and Dumfries & Galloway. This area was the birthplace of Robert the Bruce, born in 1274, at Turnberry Castle in Ayrshire where his father was the Earl of Carrick, and legend has it that William Wallace (Braveheart) was born in a small village near Kilmarnock. The area, being at the time more prosperous than its neighbours to the immediate south, was frequently invaded by the English and was home to such renowned families as the Douglases, Boyles, Crawfords and Maxwells, all of whom built impressive castles and played a part in the ongoing wars against the English.

The Duke of Buccleuch's interests include not only Drumlanrig and its 120,000 acres, but also Bowhill in the Borders, Queensberry and Langholm in the south-west, Dalkeith in Midlothian and Boughton in Northamptonshire. Much of their wealth derived from the intermarrying of the two most powerful families in southern Scotland, the Scotts (of whom Sir Walter Scott was an illustrious member) and the Douglases. There are four branches of the Douglas family, one of which is that of Drumlanrig in Nithsdale, who became the marquesses of Queensberry. Other branches of the family can trace their history back to at least the time when Sir William Douglas fought for William Wallace and a William de Douglas is recorded in the 12th century in Morayshire. By the 15th century they were considered a threat to the monarch and the 6th Earl Douglas and his brother were invited to the infamous "Black Dinner" at Edinburgh Castle with the 10-year-old King James II. They were seized and beheaded. The 8th Earl suffered the same fate in 1452, this time at the hands of King James II himself.

The Crawfords (originally Craufurd) are of Norman origin. Sir Reginald Crawford was appointed sheriff of Ayr in 1296 and his sister Margaret married Wallace of Elderslie. Their son was Sir William Wallace. Always a military family, they were staunch Jacobites but later loyal soldiers for the Hanoverian court. The family still owns Craufurdland castle. The name Maxwell seems to derive from that of a Saxon lord called Maccus, whose family had been given land and a fishery – known as *Maccus' wiel* – on the Tweed in the 12th century. The Maxwells were *Warden of the Marches* a title bestowed on John Maxwell in the mid-1500s. It meant that they were responsible for the protection of the south-western border country. Although a protestant himself John Maxwell was an ardent supporter of Mary Queen of Scots, earning the title Lord Herries. When Mary finally fled Scotland she crossed the Solway Firth, the two places of departure and landing being named to this day, Port Mary and Maryport. The famous Burrell Collection is housed in Pollok House, which was given by the Maxwells to the city of Glasgow in 1965.

The Boyle family settled in Kelburn overlooking the Firth of Clyde, in 1140; the family, then known as de Boyville, had come from Caen in Normandy in 1066. They

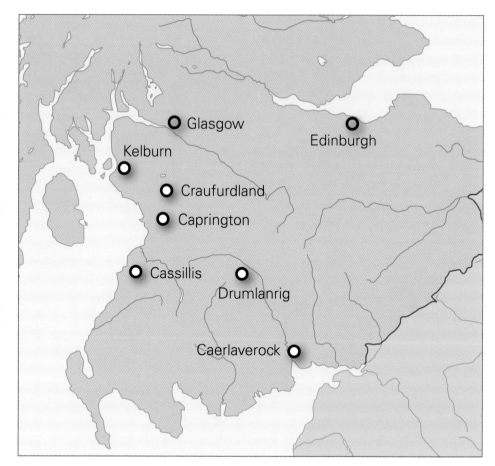

became wealthy through shipping and shipbuilding in the 17th century, earning the title Earls of Glasgow. They were strong supporters of the controversial Act of Union. Accused of bribing Jacobites to vote for the Act, they were almost certainly amongst those described by Rabbie Burns in his famous poem *A Parcel of Rogues in a Nation:*

What force or guile could not subdue
Thro' many warlike ages
Is wrought now by a coward few
For hireling traitor's wages.

We're bought and sold for English gold
Such a parcel of rogues in a nation!

Burns was born in Alloway, south of Ayr, in 1759. He was the eldest of seven sons and spent his youth working on the family's modest farm, writing his first known poem at the age of 15. It was called *My Handsome Nell* and, perhaps appropriately for a lad of his age, was about women and achohol!

Drumlanrig

Completed in the 1690s, Drumlanrig in the valley of the river Nith, is a grand renaissance country house, rather than a castle, and took twelve years to complete. It is built on the site of several earlier fortresses owned by the Douglas family, Lairds of Drumlanrig since 1388. The site has strategic importance in that it guards the route from the south into the coastal areas of Ayrshire.

The Douglases were famous for their continuing loyalty to the Scottish crown – until 1567, when Sir James Douglas fought against Mary Queen of Scots at Carberry Hill. His grandson William restored the family's good name and fortune through his support of James VI and was made Earl of Queensberry in 1633. Following the Restoration the 3rd Earl, who built the present house, was also granted the title Duke of Queensberry. Drumlanrig is now one of four homes owned by the Duke of Buccleuch and Queensberry and it houses a magnificent art collection, open to the public. The collection came to international notice in 2003 when a visitor stole a Leonardo da Vinci painting, The Madonna of the Yarnwinder. It was found, apparently undamaged, in a lawyer's office in Glasgow in October 2007. The surrounding Queensberry estate comprises over 120,000 acres of tenanted hill farms, producing beef cattle and sheep (the area being too rainy for arable crops!).

Built between 1679 and 1691 Drumlanrig has been called "the most glorious residence in the British Isles".

The north façade is a fine example of Renaissance architecture.

Drumlanrig once nestled in the depths of a forest, which was cleared and the timber sold by the 4th Duke to pay off his debts, some 200 years ago.

The clock tower bears the date 1686 and its domed roof surmounted by a crown is similar in style to the clock tower at Holyrood Palace.

Caerlaverock

Every detail has to do with defence, not decoration.

Surrounded by a double moat and hundreds of acres of marshy willow woods, Caerlaverock was built to control the south-west border between England and Scotland, which in those days was the Solway Firth. The lands incorporating Caerlaverock were granted to Sir John De Maccuswell (later – Maxwell) in 1220. He built the first castle 200 metres south of the one we see today but by the 1270s Sir John's nephew, Herbert, had started building the replacement castle that forms the core of what still stands. Building began in about 1277, and this second castle was largely complete by 1300 when Edward I invaded Galloway and successfully besieged Caerlaverock with 87 knights and 3000 men and a collection of siege engines transported to the site from all over southern Scotland and northern England. The defenders numbered fewer than 70. The castle's triangular plan is unique in Scotland, and during the siege of 1300 it was noted as being

"so strong a castle that it feared no siege... in shape it was like a shield for it has but three sides round it, with a tower at each corner... And I think that you will never see a more finely situated castle, for on one side can be seen the Irish Sea, towards the west and to the north the fair moorland, surrounded by an arm of the sea, so that no creature born can approach it on two sides without putting himself in danger of the sea. On the south side it is not easy, for there are many places difficult to get through because of woods and marshes and ditches hollowed out by the sea where it meets the river." From *The Roll of Karlaverock* (1300).

The English held the castle until 1312, with the Maxwells seemingly switching their loyalty between the English and the Scottish crowns. This led to Caerlaverock being attacked by Scottish forces culminating in the siege of 1356, when Roger Kilpatrick demolished the greater part of the building. Most of the remains of the castle today date back to the rebuilding that took place through the remainder of the 1300s and most of the 1400s. After seeing various reversals of their fortunes during the wars with the English, the Maxwells finally saw their castle ruined by the Covenantors in 1640.

The castle has stood empty since its destruction by the Covenantors in 1640.

Caerlaverock's triangular design is unique among Scottish Castles. It was completed around 1300.

The suit of armour on the staircase is a reminder of the battle of Bothwell Brig, fought nearby in 1679.

Caprington

Caprington castle was originally a property of the Wallaces of Sundrum. In 1425 the property passed to the Cunninghame (Cunnyngham) family, when Adam Cunnyngham married the daughter of Sir Duncan Wallace, and the family remain in possession of Caprington today. The Cunnynghams had settled north of Kilmarnock, Ayrshire by the end of the 13th century, though the earliest-known member of the family is Warnebald, a servant or tenant of Hugh de Moreville, who appears to have settled here in the 12th century. Hervy de Cunningham, son of the Laird of Kilmaurs, fought for Alexander III against the Norwegian invaders at the Battle of Largs in 1263. The family were supporters of the Scottish crown throughout the Wars of Independence, adding significantly to their land-holdings. However in 1448, Sir Alexander Montgomery, Sir Robert Cunnyngham's brother-in-law, was made Bailie of Cunnynghame, a title that Sir Robert Cunnyngham felt belonged to him. This event sparked the bloody Montgomery/Cunnyngham feud that lasted 213 years, ending in 1661 when William Cunnyngham, 9th Earl of Glencairn, was made Lord High Chancellor of Scotland and married Margaret Montgomery, daughter of Alexander, 6th Earl of Eglinton. In 1488 the Cunnynghams had added the title Earl of Glencairn. The 5th Earl of Glencairn was a staunch Protestant and friend of John Knox and in 1657 was one of the Scottish nobles who took the surrender of Mary Queen of Scots following the Battle of Carberry Hill. The Cunnynghams were also involved in The Plantation of Ulster, when the English sent their supporters to colonise the six northern Irish counties, by force. One result of this is that Cunningham is now among the more common of Irish family surnames.

Caprington was never specifically a military structure and much of the present appearance is a result of the alterations carried out in 1820. It is based, however, on a 14th-15th century keep with a later wing, built on a low rocky outcrop by the river Irvine. It was converted and extended in the 19th century as a castellated mansion. At this time the gardens became an important feature but clearly London sophisticates were as critical then as now of provincial taste and *The Gardener's Magazine* of 1833, noted that 'Caprington Castle has lately received great additions and a number of trees have been transplanted in the grounds according to Sir Henry Steuart's manner; but they are too much dotted instead of being grouped'.

Caprington castle is a 14th-15th century keep with a later wing, built on a low rocky outcrop by the river Irvine.

The furniture here is Jacobean but the building is predominantly 19th century.

Cassillis

Local legend has it that the king of the gypsies eloped with a Countess of Cassillis (pronounced *cassels*) and after the enraged Earl caught up with the elopers he hanged the gypsy and his followers on the Dule Tree at Cassillis Castle and imprisoned his errant spouse in nearby Maybole castle. This story does, however, seem to be totally unfounded…

Cassillis has belonged to the Kennedy family since the mid-14th century. They were great supporters of the Stewarts and earned the title Earls of Cassillis in 1509. Despite switching their allegiances back and forth between England and Scotland over subsequent centuries the family were somehow astute enough to retain their titles and their ownership of the estate. The Kennedys built Baltersan Tower, Maybole Castle and, in 1603, Greenan Castle south of Ayr, and Culzean and Dalquharran castles also belong to the family. In the 18th century Captain Archibald Kennedy settled in America. He was an officer in the Royal Navy and became the largest property owner in New York. Cassillis is however now the family home.

The name Cassillis derives from the Gaelic *caisial*, meaning fort. The castle was built in the 1300s and the walls at their base are an incredible 16-20 feet (five to six metres) thick, and are still ten feet (three metres) thick at the third floor. An unusual architectural feature of the castle is that the central newel post (the middle, supporting part) of the spiral staircase is hollow, with room enough for a man to climb up within it.

Cassillis has been in the Kennedy family since the 14th century.

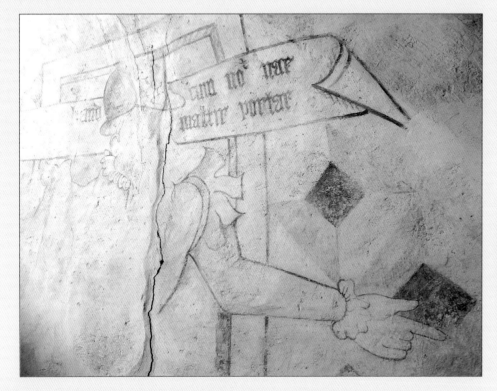

This wall-painting by the Laird's apartments dates from 1456.

Here the massive thickness of the walls can be clearly seen.

The Turnpike Stair is unusual in having a hollow newel post, large enough for a man to climb up inside it.

Dunure Castle, built in the late 1200s, was the Kennedy's first seat in Ayrshire. John Kennedy acquired lands at Cassillis and started to build the castle in the 1350s.

The haunted Countess's Room at the top of the tower has the window from which she witnessed the hanging of her lover, the gypsy king, Johnny Faa.

The main hall is part of the central tower which was added to the castle in 1825.

Craufurdland

Craufurdland is the ancestral home of the Houison Craufurds (this spelling is an old form of the more usual Crawford). The family were granted lands in the Barony of Craufurd in the 11th century, and adopted the place-name as their family name. Sir Reginald Craufurd was appointed sheriff of Ayr in 1296. His sister Margaret married Wallace of Elderslie and gave birth to the great Scottish patriot, Sir William Wallace and the Craufurds fought alongside Wallace in his struggle to remove the English occupiers from Scotland. Subsequent generations of the family remained loyal supporters of the Scottish crown, fighting at Bannockburn, Flodden, Dettingen and Fontenoy, and later in WWs I & II (in the later conflicts for Britain, not just for Scotland).

The castle's excellent defensive position, looking out over Fenwick Water makes it likely that there was an early fortification here but the oldest part of the present building probably dates from the 1500s with substantial additions in the 17th and 18th centuries. The Gothic styling was added when the castle was further enlarged in 1825.

In the *History of the County of Ayr* by Thomas George Stevenson (1856) we read "The ancient residence has been greatly augmented by recent additions, all in excellent keeping with the character of the building... The most ancient part of it, the tower, is said, although on what authority we know not, to have been *built prior to the days of William the Conqueror.*"

The right-hand section is 16th, the left 17th and the central tower 19th century.

The 1581 section of Kelburn castle can be clearly distinguished from the more recent parts of the building by its two impressive stair towers on opposite corners.

Kelburn

The entrance hall and a new wing were added in 1700, and a Victorian wing in 1879, with decoration by William Morris.

Kelburn is thought to be the oldest castle in Scotland continuously inhabited by the same family. The de Boyvilles from Caen in Normandy came over to Britain with William the Conqueror in 1066 and settled in Kelburn in 1140. A keep, designed for defence rather than comfort, was probably built by 1200 but what, if anything, remains of that original structure is now enclosed within a grander castle, the first part of which was completed in 1581 by John Boyle, who became first Baron of Fairlie that same year. The family had always been staunch supporters of the crown and the first Baron raised a force of a hundred men to fight for Mary Queen of Scots. At the same time Boyle was amassing a fortune through shipping and shipbuilding and becoming involved in public service working for Customs and Excise attempting to stamp out smuggling on the Ayrshire coast. His son David Boyle, supporter of the Glorious Revolution, was made Viscount of Kelburn, Earl of Glasgow, a Privy Counsellor and Lord of the Treasury. In the latter half of the 19th century the 6th Earl managed to run through the whole of the family's fortune and one million pounds besides, building churches and sponsoring good works all over Scotland. Though the house remains with the family it is now without the treasures that once filled its rooms. The 1581 castle can be clearly distinguished from the more recent parts of the building by its two impressive stair towers on opposite corners. The entrance hall and a new wing were added in 1700, and a Victorian wing in 1879, with decoration by William Morris.

At the end of the drive is the William and Mary wing, from 1722.

The drawing room, in the 17th century wing, added by the 1st Earl of Glasgow.

155

Photographer´s Note

What a pleasure it used to be coming back from a photographic trip with 50 rolls of film and taking them to the labs for processing. The feeling of anticipation during the two hour wait and the excitement of the return to the labs and feeling the smoothness of the sheets of film in their sleeves and putting them on the light box. The boredom on the faces of those who had processed the films having to listen to me waxing lyrical about where I had been and what I had done! The physical presence of the film displayed through transmitted light rather than on a screen through a series of digital zeros and ones.

And so I am reminded of the good old days through the publication of this book. Most of the images were shot on film. It's not that I don't like digital photography, it is just that the new world has asked so many more questions of us all than it has provided answers to.

Transparencies always gave a reference point to which one could return to see what the final printed image should look like. Their downside was the knowledge that was needed to gather good results in all conditions. The use of meters to measure colour temperature and the use of colour compensation filters. The knowledge and understanding that was needed to select the right films for the right conditions. Digital cameras seem to be able to control these issues on the computer with their software. What a luxury! I have noticed, however, that exposure is almost as critical for digital images as it ever was for creating transparencies.

The photographs contained in this book have been taken over a number of years and it has been a pleasure to re-visit the old transparencies and to take some new images with the aid of digital cameras!

A book of this nature is not just about taking photographs, it is also about meeting interesting people in diverse locations–often having to take pictures in adverse conditions. Essentially it is about getting the job done. In a number of instances I went back to make sure I got what I wanted. The second long journey to Dunvegan on the west coast of Skye was definitely worth it!!

It is 18 years ago that I first started out as a landscape photographer eighteen years ago having previously done commercial work. I have learned much in that time and the more I learn the less I know but the better equipped I have become to judge what feels right in visual terms. Photography as an art form is all about feel and instinct. Knowing what seems to be and feels right rather than being able to express it in words.

I am highly conscious of design and one of the benefits of digital image making, especially in view of the new range "live view" SLRs, is the ability to be able to see an image within a rectangle on the back of the camera.

How often did we used to remark: "…but everything looked so much smaller when I got my prints back from the labs"? Now being able to see what you are taking as a two dimensional image on the back of the camera has made people a lot more aware of the relationships of shapes within a composition. The basics of two-dimensional art is the organisation of shapes, normally within a rectangle.

An essential skill of the photographer is the ability to be able to convert what is three-dimensional visual information into a two-dimensional form. My golden rule for picture taking is being aware of the negative shapes as well as the positive ones. In two-dimensional terms both positive shapes (the objects in the picture) and negative shapes (the shapes between the objects) are of equal value. By focussing on the negative elements composition becomes much easier to control.

half title page	title page	14	15	16
Hasselblad 500CM 80mm f/8, 8 secs. Kodak EPP 100	Nikon D200 18-200mm f/13, 1/160 sec. 100 ASA	Nikon D200 18-200mm f/8, 1/125 sec. 100 ASA	Kodak DCS Pro SLR/n 28-70mm f/4.8, 1/350 sec. 160 ASA	Hasselblad 500CM 80mm f/8.5, 1/125 sec. Fuji Velvia 50

16	16	17	18	18

Nikon FE 28mm pc f/8.5, 1/125 sec. Fuji Velvia 50	Minolta 9000 35-70mm f/8.5, 1/125 sec. Fuji Velvia 50	Minolta 9000 80-200mm f/11, 1/125 sec. Fuji Velvia 50	Kodak DCS Pro SLR/n 28-70mm f/5.6, 1/180 sec. 160 ASA	Hasselblad 500CM 150mm f/8.5, 1/125 sec. Fuji Velvia 50

19	21	22	22	23
	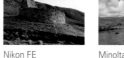			
Nikon FE 28mm pc f/8.5, 1/60 sec. Fuji Velvia 50	Minolta 9000 80-200mm f/8, 1/30 sec. Kodak EPP 100	Minolta 9000 80-200mm f/8.5, 1/30 sec. Kodak EPP 100	Minolta 9000 80-200mm f/8.5, 1/30 sec. Kodak EPP 100	Nikon FE 28mm pc f/11.5, 1/60 sec. Kodak EPP 100

24	25	26	26	27
Hasselblad 500CM 50mm f/11, 1/15 sec. Kodak EPP 100	Hasselblad 500CM 50mm f/11, 1/15 sec. Kodak EPP 100	Nikon FE 28mm pc f/11.5, 1/60 sec Kodak EPP 100	Hasselblad 500CM 50mm f/11, 1/15 sec. Kodak EPP 100	Minolta 9000 80-200mm f/5.6, 1/60 sec. Kodak EPP 100

27
Nikon FE
28mm pc
f/8, 1/8 sec.
Kodak EPP 100

27
Hasselblad 500CM
120mm
f/11, 1/125 sec.
Kodak EPP 100

28
Hasselblad SWC/M
38mm
f/11, 1/15 sec.
Kodak EPP 100

29
Nikon FE
28mm pc
f/8, 1/60 sec.
Kodak EPP 100

29
Nikon FE
28mm pc
f/11, 1/125 sec.
Kodak EPP 100

29
Hasselblad 500CM
120mm
f/11, 1/125 sec.
Kodak EPP 100

30/31
Sinar 6/12 back
47mm
f/11.5, 1/125 sec.
Kodak EPP 100

32
Nikon FE
28mm pc
f/11, 1/125 sec.
Kodak EPP 100

32
Minolta 9000
80-200mm
f/5.6, 1/8 sec.
Kodak EPP 100

32
Nikon FE
28mm pc
f/8, 1/30 sec.
Kodak EPP 100

33
Hasselblad SWC/M
38mm
f/8, 1/15 sec.
Kodak EPP 100

34/35
Sinar 6/12 back
47mm
f/11.5, 1/125 sec.
Kodak EPP 100

37
Hasselblad 500CM
50mm
f/11, 1/4 sec.
Kodak EPP 100

37
Hasselblad 500CM
120mm
f/11, 1/125 sec.
Kodak EPP 100

38
Minolta 9000
80-200mm
f/5.6, 1/125 sec.
Kodak EPP 100

38
Nikon FE
28mm pc
f/11, 1/125 sec.
Kodak EPP 100

39
Hasselblad 500CM
50mm
f/11, 1/90 sec.
Kodak EPP 100

40
Hasselblad 500CM
50mm
f/8, 1/125 sec.
Kodak EPP 10

40
Nikon FE
28mm pc
f/11, 1/8 sec.
Kodak EPP 100

40
Hasselblad 500CM
50mm
f/8, 1/15 sec.
Kodak EPP 100

41
Hasselblad 500CM
50mm
f/8, 1/4 sec.
Kodak EPP 100

42
Nikon D200
18-200mm
f/6.3, 1/125 sec.
100 ASA

42
Nikon D200
18-200mm
f/5.6, 1/80 sec.
800 ASA

42
Nikon D200
18-200mm
f/4.5, 1/20 sec.
800 ASA

42
Nikon D200
18-200mm
f/10, 2.5 sec.
100 ASA

43
Nikon D200
18-200mm
f/13, 1/160 sec.
100 ASA

44
Nikon D200
18-200mm
f/18, 1/125 sec.
100 ASA

45
Nikon D200
18-200mm
f/18, 1/125 sec.
100 ASA

45
Nikon D200
18-200mm
f/13, 1/125 sec.
100 ASA

45
Nikon D200
18-200mm
f/11, 1/125 sec.
100 ASA

45
Nikon D200
18-200mm
f/6.3, 1/30 sec.
800 ASA

46
Nikon D200
18-200mm
f/14, 1/125 sec.
100 ASA

47
Nikon D200
18-200mm
f/14, 1/125 sec.
100 ASA

48
Minolta 9000
80-200mm
f/5.6, 1/8 sec.
Kodak EPP 100

48
Minolta 9000
80-200mm
f/5.6, 1/15 sec.
Kodak EPP 100

48 ri
Nikon FE
28mm pc
f/11, 1/125 sec.
Kodak EPP 100

49
Nikon FE
28mm pc
f/11, 1/125 sec.
Kodak EPP 100

50
Hasselblad SWC/M
38mm
f/8, 1/15 sec.
Kodak EPP 100

51
Minolta 9000
80-200mm
f/5.6, 1/30 sec.
Kodak EPP 100

51
Nikon FE
28mm pc
f/5.6, 1/30 sec.
Kodak EPP 100

51
Hasselblad 500CM
50mm
f/8, 1/15 sec.
Kodak EPP 100

51
Hasselblad 500CM
50mm
f/11.5, 1/125 sec.
Kodak EPP 100

52
Hasselblad 500CM
50mm
f/8, 1/15 sec.
Kodak EPP 100

53
Hasselblad 500CM
120mm
f/8, 1/250 sec.
Kodak EPP 100

54
Hasselblad 500CM
50mm
f/8, 1/15 sec.
Kodak EPP 100

55
Nikon FE
28mm pc
f/8, 1/90 sec.
Kodak EPP 100

56
Minolta 9000
80-200mm
f/5.6, 1/30 sec.
Kodak EPP 100

57
Hasselblad 500CM
120mm
f/8, 1/125 sec.
Kodak EPP 100

57
Hasselblad 500CM
50mm
f/8, 1/60 sec.
Kodak EPP 100

57
Hasselblad 500CM
80mm
f/8, 1/15 sec.
Kodak EPP 100

57
Hasselblad 500CM
50mm
f/8, 1/125 sec.
Kodak EPP 100

58
Nikon FE
28mm pc
f/8.5, 1/125 sec.
Kodak EPP 100

59
Sinar 6/9 back
47mm
f/11.5, 1/125 sec.
Kodak EPP 100

60/61
Sinar 6/9 back
47mm
f/11.5, 1/125 sec.
Kodak EPP 100

62/63
Kodak DCS Pro SLR/n
28-70mm
f/6.7, 1/90 sec.
160 ASA

64
Nikon FE
28mm pc
f/8.5, 1/125 sec.
Kodak EPP 100

65
Minolta 9000
80-200mm
f/5.6, 1/30 sec.
Kodak EPP 100

65
Nikon FE
28mm pc
f/5.6, 1/125 sec.
Kodak EPP 100

66
Minolta 9000
80-200mm
f/5.6, 1/8 sec.
Kodak EPP 100

66
Minolta 9000
80-200mm
f/11.5, 1/90 sec.
Kodak EPP 100

66
Minolta 9000
80-200mm
F/5.6, 1/500 sec.
Kodak EPP 100

67
Sinar 6/9 back
47mm
f/8, 1/15 sec.
Kodak EPP 100

68
Nikon FE
28mm pc
f/5.6, 1/30 sec.
Kodak EPP 100

68
Minolta 9000
80-200mm
f/5.6, 1/250 sec.
Kodak EPP 100

69
Sinar 6/9 back
47mm
f/8, 1/125 sec.
Kodak EPP 100

70
Nikon FE
28mm pc
f/11, 1/30 sec.
Kodak EPP 100

71
Nikon FE
28mm pc
f/8, 1/30 sec.
Kodak EPP 100

73
Kodak DCS Pro SLR/n
28-70mm
f/5.6, 1/90 sec.
160 ASA

74
Nikon D200
18-200mm
f/9, 1/320 sec.
100 ASA

74
Nikon D200
18-200mm
f/8, 1/250 sec.
100 ASA

74
D200
18-200mm
f/10, 1/200 sec.
100 ASA

75
Nikon D200
18-200mm
f/14, 1/125 sec.
100 ASA

76
Hasselblad SWC/M
38mm
f/8, 1/8 sec.
Kodak EPP 100

77
Nikon D200
18-200mm
f/10, 1/320 sec.
100 ASA

77
Hasselblad 500CM
120mm
f/8, 1/125 sec.
Kodak EPP 100

77
Minolta 9000
80-200mm
f/8, 1/60 sec.
Kodak EPP 100

78
Hasselblad 500CM
120mm
f/11, 1/125 sec.
Kodak EPP 100

79
Minolta 9000
28-70mm
f/8, 1/30 sec.
Kodak EPP 100

79
Hasselblad 500CM
120mm
f/8.5, 1/125 sec.
Kodak EPP 100

79
Hasselblad 500CM
120mm
f/8.5, 1/125 sec.
Kodak EPP 100

80/81
Sinar 6/9
90mm
F/11.5, 1/125 sec.
Kodak EPP 100

82
Nikon FE
28mm pc
f/8, 1/15 sec.
Kodak EPP 100

82
Hasselblad 500CM
50mm
f/8, 1/125 sec.
Kodak EPP 100

83
Hasselblad SWC/M
38mm
f/11, 1/8 sec.
Kodak EPP 100

84
Kodak DCS Pro SLR/n
28-70mm
f/19, 1/60 sec.
160 ASA

84
Kodak DCS Pro SLR/n
28-70mm
f/16, 1/60 sec.
160 ASA

85
Kodak DCS Pro SLR/n
28-70mm
f/11, 1/125 sec.
160 ASA

86
Nikon FE
28mm pc
f/11, 1/125 sec.
Kodak EPP 100

87
Nikon FE
28mm pc
f/8, 1/8 sec.
Kodak EPP 100

87
Nikon FE
28mm pc
f/8, 1/15 sec.
Kodak EPP 100

87
Hasselblad 500CM
120mm
f/8.5, 1/125 sec.
Kodak EPP 100

88/89
Sinar 6/9
65 mm
F/11, 1/125 sec.
Kodak EPP 100

90
Nikon FE
28mm pc
f/8, 1/250 sec.
Kodak EPP 100

90
Minolta 9000
80-200mm
f/8, 1/30 sec.
Kodak EPP 100

91
Nikon FE
28mm pc
f/8, 1/250 sec.
Kodak EPP 100

92
Hasselblad 500CM
120mm
f/8, 8 secs.
Kodak EPP 100

93
Minolta 9000
28-70mm
f/8.5, 1/125 sec.
Fuji Velvia 50

93
Minolta 9000
28-70mm
f/11, 1/125 sec.
Fuji Velvia 50

94
Sinar 6/9
90mm
F/11.5, 1/125 sec.
Kodak EPP 100

95
Hasselblad 500CM
50mm
f/8, 1/15 sec.
Kodak EPP 100

95
Hasselblad 500CM
120mm
f/8, 1/125 sec.
Kodak EPP 100

95
Minolta 9000
80-200mm
f/11.5, 1/125 sec.
Kodak EPP 100

96
Minolta 9000
80-200mm
f/11.5, 1/125 sec.
Kodak EPP 100

96
Minolta 9000
80-200mm
f/8, 1/30 sec.
Kodak EPP 100

96
Hasselblad 500CM
120mm
f/8, 1/125 sec.
Kodak EPP 100

97
Hasselblad 500CM
50mm
f/8, 1/4 sec.
Kodak EPP 100

97
Hasselblad 500CM
50mm
f/8, 1/8 sec.
Kodak EPP 100

97
Hasselblad 500CM
50mm
f/8, 1/8 sec.
Kodak EPP 100

97
Minolta 9000
80-200mm
f/11.5, 1/125 sec.
Kodak EPP 100

98
Kodak DCS Pro SLR/n
28-70mm
f/11, 1/30 sec.
160 ASA

98
Kodak DCS Pro SLR/n
28-70mm
f/2.8, 1/45 sec.
160 ASA

99
Kodak DCS Pro SLR/n
28-70mm
f/2.8, 1/45 sec.
160 ASA

100
Hasselblad SWC/M
38mm
f/11, 1/2 sec.
Kodak EPP 100

101
Hasselblad 500CM
50mm
f/8, 1/4 sec.
Kodak EPP 100

101
Nikon FE
28mm pc
f/8, 1/15 sec.
Kodak EPP 100

101
Minolta 9000
28-70mm
f/5.6, 1/125 sec.
Kodak EPP 100

102
Nikon FE
28mm pc
f/5.6, 1/125 sec.
Kodak EPP 100

102
Minolta 9000
28-70mm
f/5.6, 1/125 sec.
Kodak EPP 100

102
Minolta 9000
80-200mm
f/5.6, 1/125 sec.
Kodak EPP 100

102
Minolta 9000
28-70mm
f/5.6, 1/60 sec.
Kodak EPP 100

103

Nikon FE
28mm pc
f/8, 1/125 sec.
Kodak EPP 100

104

Hasselblad 500CM
120mm
f/8, 1/125 sec.
Kodak EPP 100

104

Hasselblad 500CM
50mm
f/8, 1/15 sec.
Kodak EPP 100

104

Minolta 9000
80-200mm
f/5.6, 1/90sec.
Kodak EPP 100

105

Nikon FE
28mm pc
f/8.5, 1/125 sec.
Kodak EPP 100

106

Hasselblad 500CM
50mm
f/8, 1/15 sec.
Kodak EPP 100

107

Hasselblad 500CM
80mm
f/8, 1/15 sec.
Kodak EPP 100

109

Nikon FE
28mm pc
f/8.5, 1/125 sec.
Kodak EPP 100

109

Linhof 6/17
90mm
f/11, 1/30 sec.
Fuji Velvia 50

110

Nikon FE
28mm pc
f/8, 1/60 sec.
Kodak EPP 100

110

Kodak DCS Pro SLR/n
28-70mm
f/4.8, 1/350 sec.
160 ASA

110

Nikon FE
28mm pc
f/8, 1/90 sec.
Kodak EPP 100

111

Nikon FE
28mm pc
f/8.5, 1/125 sec.
Kodak EPP 100

112/113

Nikon FE
28mm pc
f/8, 1/250 sec.
Kodak EPP 100

114

Hasselblad 500CM
50mm
f/8, 1/8 sec.
Kodak EPP 100

115

Hasselblad 500CM
50mm
f/8, 1/15 sec.
Kodak EPP 100

115

Minolta 9000
80-200mm
f/5.6, 1/250 sec.
Kodak EPP 100

115

Nikon FE
28mm pc
f/8, 1/8 sec.
Kodak EPP 100

115

Hasselblad 500CM
120mm
f/8, 1/125 sec.
Kodak EPP 100

116

Hasselblad 500CM
150mm
f/8, 1/60 sec.
Kodak EPP 100

117

Nikon FE
28mm pc
f/11, 1/125 sec.
Kodak EPP 100

117

Hasselblad 500CM
120mm
f/8, 1/125 sec.
Kodak EPP 100

117

Minolta 9000
80-200mm
f/11, 1/125 sec.
Kodak EPP 100

117

Hasselblad 500CM
50mm
f/11, 1/125 sec.
Kodak EPP 100

118

Hasselblad 500CM
50mm
f/8, 1/8 sec.
Kodak EPP 100

119

Nikon FE
28mm pc
f/11.5, 1/125 sec.
Kodak EPP 100

121

Minolta 9000
28-70mm
f/11, 1/125 sec.
Fuji Velvia 50

122

Hasselblad 500CM
80mm
f/11, 1/125 sec.
Kodak EPP 100

123

Hasselblad 500CM
50mm
f/8, 1/60 sec.
Kodak EPP 100

123

Hasselblad 500CM
50mm
f/8, 1/4 sec.
Kodak EPP 100

123

Hasselblad 500CM
50mm
f/8, 1/125 sec.
Kodak EPP 100

124

Minolta 9000
28-70mm
f/11, 1/15 sec.
Kodak EPP 100

124

Minolta 9000
28-70mm
f/11, 1/15 sec.
Kodak EPP 100

124

Hasselblad 500CM
50mm
f/8, 1/125 sec.
Kodak EPP 100

124

Hasselblad 500CM
120mm
f/8, 1/125 sec.
Kodak EPP 100

125

Hasselblad 500CM
50mm
f/8, 1/15 sec.
Kodak EPP 100

126

Hasselblad 500CM
80mm
f/8, 1/15 sec.
Kodak EPP 100

126

Hasselblad 500CM
50mm
f/8, 1/30 sec.
Kodak EPP 100

127

Sinar 6/9
47mm
f/11.5, 1/125 sec.
Kodak EPP 100

128

Sinar 6/9
65mm
f/16, 1/125 sec.
Fuji Velvia 50

130

Nikon FE
28mm pc
f/11, 1/125 sec.
Kodak EPP 100

131

Hasselblad 500CM
50mm
f/16, 1/125 sec.
Kodak EPP 100

131

Hasselblad 500CM
50mm
f/11, 1/4 sec.
Kodak EPP 100

131

Hasselblad 500CM
120mm
f/11, 1/125 sec.
Kodak EPP100

132

Minolta 9000
28-70mm
f/5.6, 1/30 sec.
Kodak EPP 100

132

Nikon FE
28mm pc
f/11, 1/125 sec.
Kodak EPP 100

132

Minolta 9000
28-70mm
f/5.6, 1/30 sec.
Kodak EPP 100

133

Nikon FE
28mm pc
f/11, 1/60 sec.
Kodak EPP 100

134

Hasselblad 500CM
150mm
f/8, 1/125 sec.
Fuji Velvia 50

135

Minolta 9000
80-200mm
f/16, 1/125 sec.
Fuji Velvia 50

136/137

Hasselblad 500CM
120mm
f/8, 1/125 sec.
Fuji Velvia 50

138

Nikon FE
28mm pc
f/11, 1/30 sec.
Fuji Velvia 50

139

Nikon FE
28mm pc
f/8, 1/60 sec.
Fuji Velvia 50

139

Nikon FE
28mm pc
f/11, 1/60 sec.
Fuji Velvia 50

141

Nikon FE
28mm pc
f/11, 1/125 sec.
Kodak EPP 100

141

Nikon FE
28mm pc
f/11, 1/60 sec.
Kodak EPP 100

142

Nikon FE
28mm pc
f/11, 1/125 sec.
Kodak EPP 100

143

Minolta 9000
80-200mm
f/8, 1/125 sec.
Fuji Velvia 50

144

Kodak DCS Pro SLR/n
28-70mm
f/11, 1/30 sec.
160 ASA

144

Kodak DCS Pro SLR/n
28-70mm
f/4.8, 1/60 sec.
160 ASA

145

Kodak DCS Pro SLR/n
28-70mm
f/5.6, 1/180 sec.
160 ASA

146

Hasselblad SWC/M
38mm
f/11, 1/2 sec.
Kodak EPP 10

147

Nikon FE
28mm pc
f/8.5, 1/125 sec.
Kodak EPP 100

147

Hasselblad SWC/M
38mm
f/11, 1/15 sec.
Kodak EPP 100

148

Hasselblad 500CM
50mm
f/8, 1/125 sec.
Kodak EPP 100

148

Hasselblad 500CM
50mm
f/8, 1/8 sec.
Kodak EPP 100

148

Hasselblad 500CM
50mm
f/16, 1/125 sec.
Kodak EPP 100

149

Hasselblad 500CM
50mm
f/11, 1/125 sec.
Kodak EPP 100

150

Hasselblad 500CM
50mm
f/11, 1/125 sec.
Kodak EPP 100

151

Nikon FE
28mm pc
f/11, 1/125 sec.
Kodak EPP 100

152

Hasselblad SWC/M
38mm
f/11, 1/15 sec.
Kodak EPP 100

153

Nikon FE
28mm pc
f/11, 16 sec.
Kodak EPP 100

153

Hasselblad 500CM
50mm
f/11, 1/30 sec.
Kodak EPP 100

153

Hasselblad 500CM
50mm
f/11, 1/8 sec.
Kodak EPP 100

154

Nikon FE
28mm pc
f/11, 1/125 sec.
Kodak EPP 100

155

Hasselblad 500CM
50mm
f/11, 1/4 sec.
Kodak EPP 100

155

Hasselblad 500CM
50mm
f/11, 1/8sec.
Kodak EPP 100

155

Nikon FE
28mm pc
f/8, 1/125 sec.
Kodak EPP 100

pagenumber

camera
lens
aperture, exp. time
film/ASA

Glossary

Ashlar: finely-trimmed stone blocks used in construction of high-quality walls

Bailey: outer wall and courtyard of a castle

Barbican: a tower projecting from a wall, normally over the gateway of a castle

Barmkin: the stone wall surrounding a tower-house or keep

Bartizan: a projecting gallery in a castle wall, or a corbelled corner turret

Bastion: a projecting structure in a defensive or curtain wall often with the shape of a sharp point, from which defenders of a castle can deal with attackers while remaining protected

Batter or Battering: the slope of a castle wall designed to enable it to absorb some of the force of artillery bombardment

Bombard: an early 15th century heavy cannon

Bretasche: the wooden covered walkway set high on and projecting out beyond the castle walls

Broch: an Iron-Age dry-stone-walled early domestic or defensive structure, found throughout Scotland

Corbel: the supporting stonework for a structure, such as a small tower, projecting from a castle wall

Crannog: a fortified island in a loch

Crenellations: battlements, on top of the outer walls

Donjon: the fortified central tower comprising the lord's residence: derivation of the modern word *dungeon*, which means something quite different

Embrasure: the opening in a wall, wider on the inside than the outside, allowing the defender a wide angle through which to fire at attackers

Fortalice: any small fort or defensive structure

Fosse: a moat or defensive ditch

Keep: the strong tower at the centre of the castle complex

Machicolation: the structure at the top of a castle's walls, supported on corbels, with spaces through which defenders could drop objects onto attackers below them

Motte: a mound of earth on which a wooden structure is built

Pale or Palisade: a strong fence built of stakes or tree-trunks

Peel: an enclosure surrounded by a wooden palisade

Reiver: a robber, thief or "raider"

Yett: a secure iron gate used in conjunction with a wooden door to defend the entry point to a castle

Acknowledgements

I would like to thank the castle owners for allowing us to take photographs in and around their beautiful homes. Thanks to the National Trust for Scotland for Brodie, Crathes, and Craigievar Castles and to Historic Scotland who perform such an important function in helping to preserve Scotland's built heritage.

Thanks to author and publisher Cameron Brown for giving me yet another opportunity to get my photographs into print. Thanks to Niki for all his design work which has perhaps made some of my pictures appear better than they really are! Thanks again to Ditz for her editorial eye and support.

Finally, but very importantly, Cameron and I must thank Hugh Cantlie, whose book *Ancestral Castles of Scotland* (Collins & Brown) first enabled me to become involved in photographing so many of these privately-owned castles, and to whose knowledge of the subject Cameron admits to being indebted!

This book is dedicated to Katy, Amy and Timothy.

Sampson Lloyd, 2008